disabled children in a society at war

A Casebook from Bosnia

Rachel Hastie

Oxfam UK and Ireland

facing page Gorazde, Bosnia-Hercegovina: the impact of shell-fire on a residential area

Published by Oxfam UK and Ireland
First published 1997

© Oxfam UK and Ireland 1997

A catalogue record for this publication is available from the British Library.

ISBN 0 85598 373 6

Published by Oxfam UK and Ireland, 274 Banbury Road, Oxford OX2 7DZ, UK
(registered as a charity, no. 202918)

Available in Ireland from Oxfam in Ireland, 19 Clanwilliam Terrace, Dublin 2 (tel. 01 661 8544). Addresses of agents and distributors are given on the last page.

Designed by Oxfam Design Department OX416/RB/97
Printed by Oxfam Print Unit

Oxfam UK and Ireland is a member of Oxfam International.

Front cover photo: Howard Davies/Oxfam

UNHCR

Contents

below Izudin Salihovic, living in a collective centre in Tuzla in 1994. His home village of Bratunac was burned down two years previously.

Oxfam/Bill Stephenson

Introduction

The dramatic changes in Eastern Europe over the last few years have brought aid agencies into new territories to face new challenges. Although Oxfam (UK and Ireland) began its existence distributing aid in mainland Europe following World War II, much of its work over the past 50 years has been in Asia and the Middle East, Africa, and Latin America. The decision to begin work in a whole new area was not an easy one: budgets, staff, and resources were stretched to cope with existing demands; lack of long-term financial stability had been a continual problem; and as an organisation Oxfam (UK and Ireland) [hereafter referred to as 'Oxfam'] lacked experience and knowledge of working in this new region. Despite these drawbacks, in 1992 Oxfam began working in Albania, Former Yugoslavia, and the Former Soviet Union, distributing humanitarian aid where needed, as well as working on longer-term development projects.

Because this is such a new area of work, there has so far been little evaluation or analysis to contribute to the agency's own learning. This casebook is not an evaluation in the formal sense. Its purpose is to examine a particular experience and from that draw lessons for the future. It is primarily about the Koraci Nade ('Steps of Hope') Centre for disabled children, an Oxfam project in Bosnia-Hercegovina. Koraci Nade is one of a number of projects with disabled people which together make up Oxfam's disability programme in Bosnia. The purpose of developing an approach based on an integrated programme (as opposed to one consisting of unrelated projects) is to ensure that disability is addressed at all levels. A whole range of projects and actions makes up the programme; they include centres such as Koraci Nade; the translation of books; local, national, and international advocacy work; training seminars and workshops; and so on. In line with this programme-based approach, this book will consider the individual project in a wider context, examining factors such as the effects of the conflict in Bosnia; the situation of disabled adults; policy and practice on disability issues within Oxfam; and social and institutional discrimination.

The Koraci Nade Centre in Tuzla, northern Bosnia, offers special support for disabled children, with a principal emphasis on development through play. The centre has undergone considerable change in its internal structure since it opened, and the dramatic changes in the external environment have also made a huge impact on it. The Koraci Nade Centre will be considered in detail in the first part of the book, but two other associated projects in Tuzla feature strongly in the text. The ZID workshop makes seating units for children with cerebral palsy, in conjunction with the Koraci Nade Centre; and in the Lotos Resource Centre, disabled adults plan services in legal advice, training, computing, foreign languages, sewing, knitting, and advocacy on basic rights.

Each project exists within a wider context, which influences what it is able to achieve and the approach that should be taken: every intervention is affected by, and affects, conditions that prevail in the community. Using examples from the Koraci Nade project and associated work with disabled people in Bosnia, the later chapters of this casebook examine some of the wider issues for work on disability.

The fourth chapter was not part of the original plan for this book. It has emerged in response to a growing awareness that any organisation promoting change has to begin with itself — its structures, policy, and practice. This issue was raised so frequently during my interviews with Oxfam staff and partners for this book that it clearly needed a chapter of its own. The text documents a continuing process which has been sensitive and difficult for many of those involved. The experience of the Oxfam Tuzla team in facing up to their own prejudices and trying to find ways to deal with them will, it is hoped, help others to address disablism and start to take practical measures to eradicate it and other forms of discrimination within their own institutions.

Following this analysis of change within internal systems, the fifth chapter examines the 'social model' of disability and the difficulties and opportunities encountered when Oxfam tried to introduce this approach into the Bosnian context. The social model assumes a particular set of roles for the State, the community, and the individual, but can it be transferred from its origins in countries characterised by democratic systems and an active civil society to countries like Bosnia which are in transition from a more collectivist system of values? This issue is very relevant to work with disabled people in Eastern Europe.

The sixth chapter considers how disability work is affected by civil and military conflict, and how aid projects in such contexts affect disabled people. The way in which non-government organisations (NGOs) analyse the environment in which they work is their basis for decision-making about target groups and types of intervention. Yet whatever we do affects not only the target group we have chosen, but the community as a whole. In effect, by choosing to work with some people, we are by default effectively choosing not to work with others. In times of conflict, disability becomes increasingly politicised, and relationships between different groups in society change. This is especially so when there is competition for resources between military and civilian groups, and between people disabled by the war and those disabled before the war. The analysis and assumptions we make about the context in which we work have far-reaching effects, and often we are not even aware of this until it is too late. Conflict can also be a catalyst for change, as we shall see.

Aid agencies continually debate to what extent developmental work can be carried out during an emergency. Increasingly, agencies such as Oxfam find themselves working in disputed territories, and in long-running conflicts that can last for years, even decades. Chapter 7 examines the relationship between short-term emergency work to meet immediate needs and long-term development work to help people to fulfil their potential, using examples of Oxfam's experience of working in conflict in Bosnia.

The final chapter summarises the main learning points identified by all who have contributed to this book, and examines what future there is for the Koraci Nade children's centre.

Notes on the text

The Koraci Nade project raises some general points about disability that are relevant to all aid agencies, and to all emergency and development workers. This casebook is written for development workers and students of development studies, rather than rehabilitation professionals or therapists. It should be most useful to those who have to manage programmes without much knowledge or experience of working on disability issues. Rehabilitation workers and therapists have a range of professional resources to draw on in their work with disabled people, but this book's treatment of the broader issues of an organisational approach may be useful to them. Any one of the staff of Koraci Nade would have written a very different book, and indeed may do so some day. This book is not a practical manual, but explores issues while trying to stay grounded in the practical experiences of Koraci Nade and Oxfam in Tuzla.

When I started writing this casebook, I had just finished working as Oxfam's Deputy Country Representative in Bosnia. It has been a great learning experience for me to look in depth at a project with which I had been associated for the previous 18 months. However, working on the book within a very limited time frame meant that I have had to be selective about the amount of information I could include. To some extent, this book is a result of its time frame. Another limitation has been that some people whose contributions would have been very welcome and useful have been unable to contribute to the book, for a number of reasons.

The text that follows is based on my experience of working in Bosnia during 1995 and 1996; it includes my own observations, experiences, and anecdotal material. Other material was collected during a brief, but intensive, period of research in October and November 1996. Transcripts from many of the interviews and discussions held at that time appear in the text. Another source of material has been the Oxfam Tuzla filing system, which tells a fascinating story of the development of work on disability within the Tuzla team, and documents many of the struggles of the team as they attempted to address their own disablism.

The Koraci Nade children's centre was opened in June 1994, when Oxfam's programme was limited to the Tuzla region in north-eastern Bosnia. At that time there was virtually no contact between the Serb-held and the government-held parts of Bosnia. Not only were civilian communities unable to communicate, but aid workers also found it difficult to obtain accurate information about the 'other side'. The local media were full of the propaganda and mis-information of war, and the international media followed their own agenda, too often presenting an oversimplified picture of Bosnian Muslims as tragic helpless victims and Serbs as the perpetrators of all evil.

Oxfam was already operational in the eastern enclaves of Bosnia from its Belgrade base in neighbouring Serbia, and in November 1995 opened a permanent office in Banja Luka, followed by an office in Bijeljina in 1996. As communication lines opened up, links between Oxfam field staff and partners across the boundary dividing Bosnia have increased our knowledge of what happened during the war, and the current situation in each entity. The complex political situation and divisions in the international aid effort mean that there are significant differences in the experiences of people living in each entity. The reader must keep in mind that the analysis of myself and other contributors is primarily informed by our experiences in a part of Bosnia controlled by the Bosnian government. Oxfam's early analysis of the situation and subsequent action-planning were similarly restricted by the physical isolation and lack of information from many areas — although this gradually changed after the Dayton Peace Agreement in November 1995.

Rather than operating its own projects, Oxfam usually works with local partner organisations in development work, and in relief and emergency assistance when appropriate. However, in Bosnia the lack of local partners in the form of independent local NGOs left Oxfam with no choice but to run operational projects, while emphasising support for the development of Bosnian NGOs. Oxfam field staff assessed, planned, and implemented almost all projects themselves. This explains the 'hands-on' relationship between the office staff and the Koraci Nade project. It was a situation common to many Eastern European countries, where a lack of suitable partners made operational projects a necessity. In Bosnia the presence of a large number of international NGOs, primarily focused on emergency-relief work, has created some confusion. While these organisations represent a small fraction of the many and diverse NGOs in their own countries, they are the only role models available to Bosnian NGOs. This fact influenced the development of the local NGO sector in Bosnia, which had a very strong tendency to be relief-orientated; it even fostered the idea that NGOs will not be a necessary part of the post-war structure.

Acknowledgements

In researching this book I have been given valuable assistance by many Oxfam staff, partners, and friends in Bosnia. Amela Sulic translated, researched, and interviewed with me; Alex Jones, Usha Kar, Dinka Masic, and Alma Subic from Oxfam Bosnia read and re-read the various drafts, as did Jacqui Christy, Fiona Gell, Helen Lee, Gordana Rajkovic, and Tony Vaux. Catherine Robinson, who edited the book, gave tremendous support, both professionally and personally. I acknowledge my debt to them all, and also to colleagues in the Lotos Centre, especially Edina Barjaktarevic, Jasmin Hermes, and Kaca Sarihodzic; to the ZID workshop — Denis Jusufi, Mustafa Kladnjakovic, Sead Korabegovic, Ferid Mesic, and Muhamed Selimovic; and to Faruk Sabanovic from the Centre for Self-Reliance in Sarajevo.

In particular I must acknowledge those people who have worked so hard and in such difficult conditions to make Koraci Nade the success it is today: Cimeta Hatibovic and Muba Sarijlic, who originally opened the centre; Lisa Gilliam, Barbara Jennings-Jayaram, Helen Lee, and Alma Subic, all past Oxfam staff who helped to establish and run the centre; the Koraci Nade staff: Azra Begtasagovic, Dana Hukic, Fata Ibralic, Ajsa Mahmugtagic, Nevzeta Salihovic, Mustafa Salihovic, Fikret Selman, and Jasmina Suljagic — who endlessly impressed and inspired me with their energy, dedication, and creativity. Most importantly, I thank the children and parents of the Koraci Nade Centre, too numerous to mention individually. Many thanks too to all our friends and colleagues in the Overseas Development Administration of the UK government, which has provided substantial funding for this project and shown great understanding of the difficult circumstances under which it has existed and developed. Finally, I thank Andrea Placidi: the Koraci Nade Centre brought us together, and the story of the project in the last year parallels the story of our becoming a family; our baby Joshua Cesare arrived on the same day that the final text of the book was delivered.

Notes on language

Initial Oxfam Tuzla field staff reports sometimes used terminology about disability which Oxfam as an organisation does not consider appropriate or correct. The way in which the language of the reports changed over time mirrors the way in which each individual developed an understanding of the social model of disability. The original text of these reports has not been edited for the sake of ideological correctness: the development of an awareness of language and terminology is also part of this story and the learning process.

The terms 'mentally retarded' and 'the disabled' are not considered appropriate in English any more, but are still commonly used in many other countries. The term 'learning difficulty' is very difficult to translate into Bosnian/Serbo-Croat. Some of the people interviewed were speaking English as a foreign language and have been quoted directly — although, aware of the connotations of certain terms, they would probably have used a different word in their native language. Expressions such as 'invalid' and 'defectologist' (denoting a Bosnian profession concerned with the special education of disabled children) are common terms used in Bosnia, and there are few alternatives in the Bosnian/Serbo-Croat language which would make sense and be generally understood.

For geographical areas I have used the terms commonly used by the media and international community. 'Bosnia' is used to refer to Bosnia-Hercegovina; and the two constituent entities of Bosnia are referred to as 'the Federation' (the mainly Muslim-Croat Bosnian Federation), and 'the Republika Srpska' (the mainly Serb part of Bosnia). When writing about Oxfam's work in Bosnia, for the main part I am referring to the work of Oxfam Tuzla (which covered Tuzla Canton and Sarajevo) until late 1995, when Oxfam expanded its operations into other areas of Bosnia.

One of the greatest challenges in writing this book has been trying to achieve a balance between providing some essential background information and avoiding getting caught up in a political and military analysis. If readers want more detailed background information about the war in Bosnia, they should easily find it in any number of recently published texts. Suggestions for further reading about Bosnia, about the social model of disability, and about working in the context of armed conflict are listed at the end of the book.

Rachel Hastie
Rome
February 1997

Setting the scene   I

The war in Bosnia

The wars in Former Yugoslavia broke out in June 1991 as, one by one, the member states of the Yugoslav Federation began to declare their independence, each declaration prompting the next. In Bosnia, where all eyes were watching the erupting conflict in neighbouring Croatia, the referendum of February 1992 saw Bosnian Croats and Bosnian Muslims overwhelmingly voting for independence from Serbia and the rest of Yugoslavia. Bosnian Serb voters, on the whole, stayed at home on the instructions of the Serb leadership. Just days after the referendum, the Belgrade-controlled Yugoslav National Army started setting up road blocks across Bosnia, and war was inevitable.

The years of conflict which followed left Western Europe in a state of shock. Many Eastern European countries were emerging from communist rule after the end of the Cold War, but it was unthinkable that such a devastating and bloody conflict could break out so close to home. Moreover, Yugoslavia's more relaxed style of communism, evolving during the years of President Tito, had allowed relative freedom to its citizens. Yugoslavs went shopping in Italy and Austria, and tourists from Western European countries enjoyed Yugoslavia's Croatian coastline with numerous islands, nudist beaches, bars and night-clubs. Suddenly the tourist-brochure pictures of island beaches were replaced by television images of tanks, soldiers, burning cars, and civilians packing up to leave.

The events of the following years are well known: 'ethnic cleansing', siege, displacement, and death. Serbs fled to the northern and eastern Serbian-controlled areas of Bosnia, while Muslims and Croats fled west and south. To compound the chaos, the period of conflict between Muslims and Croats — who began as allies, turned into enemies, and then again became uneasy allies under the Bosnian Federation — reduced cities such as Mostar to ruins.

The war in Bosnia left a quarter of a million people dead and hundreds of thousands of people displaced. Here as elsewhere, following a pattern that has developed since World War II, much of the military action took place in civilian areas, with very high numbers of civilian casualties. Many of the injured became permanently disabled.

Some of the displaced were able to make their way to third countries, in Western Europe and farther afield. Their status in exile rarely gave them rights to establish a future in their host country. However, their prospects back home were infinitely worse. The people of Sarajevo lived under siege, surrounded by the better-armed and strategically placed Bosnian Serb Army. In towns such as Gorazde and Srebrenica, the population lived under almost constant shell fire for most of the war, with the Bosnian Serb Army controlling all movements in and out. There were reports of people resorting to eating straw and grass; amputations were carried out without anaesthetic; and the few medical staff who remained in these areas were exhausted.

Although the United Nations had declared six 'safe areas' in government-controlled areas of Bosnia (populated mainly by ethnic Muslims and Croats), their limited mandate and resources meant that UNPROFOR (the UN Protection Force) could do little to ensure the safety of these areas. The destruction of villages where the world's press was not witness to events included some appalling abuses of human rights. Thousands of people fled to the so-called 'safe' areas, to live in terrible conditions under shell fire and sniping. When Srebrenica, one of these 'safe' areas, fell to the Bosnian Serb Army in July 1995, thousands of men went missing — despite the UN presence — and only now are their mass graves being excavated. Another 'safe' area was Tuzla, where Oxfam began its work in Bosnia in 1993. Except for lulls in the fighting during the bitterly cold winters, the town came under frequent shell fire and people regularly died in the streets on their way to work or to buy food.

In Tuzla, as in many other Bosnian towns, thousands of displaced people — many from cities controlled by the 'other side' and from rural areas — were packed into schools and sports halls and other large buildings which were known as 'collective centres', where conditions were poor, and privacy an impossible luxury. In the Muslim-Croat Federation, many collective centres have now closed: displaced people have been moved into private houses, especially along the devastated former front lines, where their first job will be reconstruction. Across Eastern Bosnia, displaced Serbs are living in very poor sanitary conditions in overcrowded collective centres under the care of local authorities which have no resources to deal with their problems. A deep-rooted prejudice among urban people, who regard rural people as uncultured and lacking in social skills, is a major block to the integration of displaced people into their new communities. The frequent movement of displaced people from one area to another also limits the opportunities for integration and interrupts schooling and employment.

Towns such as Mostar, Gorazde, and Sarajevo suffered terrible physical damage to buildings, communications, and utilities such as water systems, besides influxes of refugees from surrounding areas. Others were less damaged,

Oxfam/Mark Allison

Oxfam/Bill Stephenson

above Mostar was shelled four or five times a day when the war was at its height.

left A collective centre in Tuzla, 1994: new trainers (supplied by Oxfam) for 10-year Izudin and his friend Raza. Twenty-three people lived in one room at this centre.

but still struggled with populations which more than doubled in size during the war. As people fled the fighting, hundreds of thousands arrived exhausted in 'secure' towns with very few belongings; the majority of them were women, children, the elderly, and the sick. Travel was severely restricted; permission was needed from the army to move more than a few kilometres out of any town, and usually denied to men of military age and professionally trained people such as doctors. Young men on all sides were picked up in the streets to be mobilised for the army; many slept in different houses each night to elude the military police. Professionals such as health workers, teachers, and psychologists were also mobilised into service in support of troops at the front lines.

With no salaries from the factories and State companies, no effective welfare service, and some of the key functions of the State replaced by the international aid effort, many people resorted to private means to survive. As in any war, the black market was a lucrative source of income for those who controlled it, and sometimes a lifeline (with a high price) for those who bought from it. Others set out blankets on street corners with their few possessions laid out for sale, hoping to raise enough cash for the day's food. Aid workers heard frequent stories of young girls in Sarajevo being paid less than £1 for sex. A packet of cigarettes or a kilo of salt cost £40 in Srebrenica, and teachers received a monthly State salary of less than £5 — whenever it was paid, which was not often. If State employees left their jobs (even though there was no work to do), they surrendered all the promised benefits of their 'jobs for life'.

Young, educated, urban Bosnians able to speak passable English found jobs with aid agencies or UNPROFOR as a way to support their entire families. They received a salary worth up to 80 times a monthly pension, and often a UN 'Blue Card', which allowed greater freedom of movement and the support of international staff, who brought in food and messages. Others benefited from the international presence by renting their homes to aid workers, often moving their entire families into the basement. The women of these families cooked, cleaned, and washed clothes for their aid-agency tenants, who in their turn used their much greater mobility to bring in food from neighbouring Croatia and were a vital source of information about the wider situation.

Finally, after three and a half years and over 30 cease-fires, some lasting only hours, the war in Bosnia ended in November 1995, when the Dayton Accords were agreed by representatives of the warring parties. The former front lines became boundaries between the two entities of Bosnia-Hercegovina: the Republika Srpska and the mainly Muslim-Croat Federation. Although the fighting has stopped, and the situation has improved dramatically for many people in Bosnia, there are large numbers of vulnerable people who are still struggling to cope with the after-effects of the war.

14

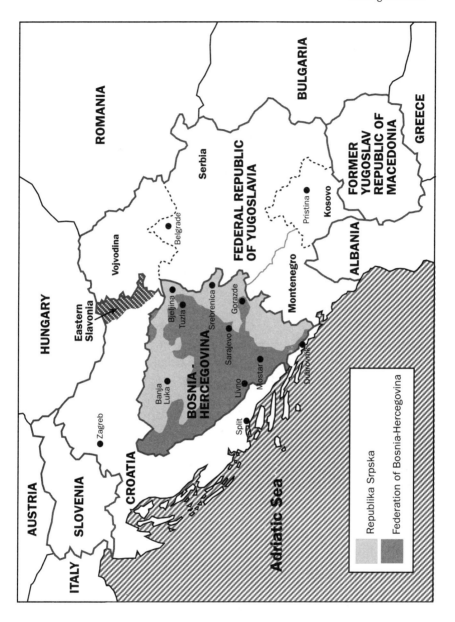

above A map of the former Yugoslavia and surrounding countries (boundaries as at September 1996)

The most vulnerable people

The general population of Bosnia had lived in relative affluence before the war, and they were hit very badly by the disintegration of Yugoslavia and the breakdown of the systems which had supported their lifestyle. For those who were in a more vulnerable position before the war, the situation was very dire indeed, and often life-threatening. Some of the most vulnerable people were the elderly, disabled people, people with medical conditions or illnesses, the mentally ill, and those who had always lived at the margins of society, such as the Romany community. The break-up of families and the community or neighbourhood support system created a whole new group of especially vulnerable people: the displaced, single-parent families, ethnic minorities, the war-injured, and those who simply could not cope psychologically with the devastation of the war.

Elderly people who had lived with their families, or were supported by a network of relatives, had to be left behind if younger family members managed to leave the country. Sometimes they were trapped on the wrong side of the front line or isolated from their relatives, stranded in a city with no roads in or out. The State pension was rarely paid, and amounted to less than £5 a month when it was paid — impossible for anyone to live on. Male family members were mobilised to the front line, with little or no pay, and away from home for long periods of time. The traditional breadwinners and protectors of the Bosnian family were gone.

The system that had allowed urban women considerable freedom to pursue an education and career and to study and travel abroad had collapsed. Rural women, who once could have coped and provided for their families if they had land in a village, were displaced into unfamiliar urban settings. Large areas of fertile land became battle zones or were mined. Young women without a male family member present were vulnerable to exploitation when dealing with the figures of authority who controlled resources vital to their well-being. Displaced women often cared for elderly relatives as well as their children; but many of the elderly, sick, and disabled were either left behind or died during the arduous journey to safety. Women became the primary providers and protectors of the family. Research commissioned by Oxfam in 1996 concluded that almost 30,000 people are missing in Bosnia; they are mainly men, leaving the legacy of thousands of female-headed households.

As the health-care system deteriorated, barely able to cope with the war-injured, people with long-term illnesses and medical conditions did not receive the treatment they needed. International sanctions against Serbia affected supplies to Serb-held parts of Bosnia, even though essential medical supplies should have been getting through. Before the Washington Agreement of 1994, which ended the war between Muslims and Croats, many Muslim-controlled areas of Bosnia were blockaded, with no port of entry except through Croatia. During the war, some people needing emergency treatment were lucky enough to get a medical evacuation through international efforts; but many more did not. Those who needed medication for conditions such as epilepsy, diabetes, and heart conditions, or treatment for cancer, heart attacks, or strokes, relied on medical aid which often simply could not meet the need. Having relatives abroad increased the chances of getting essential drugs; having friends in the international community (civilian or military) was often the only way of getting anything into Bosnia. Aid workers constantly carried mail and parcels in and out of the country.

In institutions such as psychiatric hospitals, staff members sometimes left suddenly without notice; supplies of food, clothing, and linen diminished and then disappeared. There were reports of people who had been totally dependent on their now-absent carers wandering the streets barefoot and in their night-clothes.

Pre-war Bosnia had the most multi-ethnic and integrated population in Yugoslavia. Serbs married Croats, their children married Muslims. It is difficult to find any extended family where all members belong to a single ethnic group. However, pressure from leaders who manufactured ethnic tensions to achieve their own ends forced many to abandon parts of their family, hide their ethnicity, or separate and flee to opposite sides of the front line. Ethnic minorities all over Bosnia were subject to discrimination and abuse, verbal or physical attacks. Numerous testimonies report that, in the Federation, children of mixed parentage or Serb families were beaten at school and suffered daily torment and discrimination, which they could not understand. Their former school-friends ostracised them, and abusive graffiti were painted on their homes. Serbs lost their jobs and homes, had their cars burned, or were victims of crimes which the police were reluctant to investigate, thereby legitimising further criminal acts against minority groups. In the areas where Muslims and Croats had been fighting, the signing of the Washington Agreement could not overnight negate the power of the propaganda that had brought Muslims and Croats to war. After brutal fighting it was impossible to go back to being allies with any level of mutual trust, and today the Muslim-Croat Federation remains shaky and subject to spontaneous eruptions of conflict.

The international media exposed maltreatment of Bosnian Muslims and Bosnian Croats in the Serb-held areas; many were abused, beaten, held in detention camps, expelled, or simply disappeared. As anarchy broke out, members of the military and the police perpetrated acts of violence and other abuses against unprotected civilians. Civilian gangs targeted minorities, stole their possessions, took their homes, and threw them into the streets. Males from minority groups were routinely jailed; some were mobilised into the army and then put to work digging front-line trenches under fire, with no protection or weapons. With the traditional protectors of the family gone, women were subject to sexual violence, with no place to escape to, and no one to protect their rights. Even in exile they were vulnerable to harassment, rape, and abuse by the authorities who controlled the camps and collective centres — the very people who, they hoped, would protect them.

Disability in Bosnia

Oxfam found that disabled people in particular were neglected by both the aid effort and the government. The term 'disabled people' can apply to children, teenagers, single parents, widows, and those trying to trace missing relatives; people from ethnic minorities, elderly people, and people who are mentally ill. While most disabled people are not ill, some may have medical needs because of their impairment. Injured and disabled soldiers had first claim on the

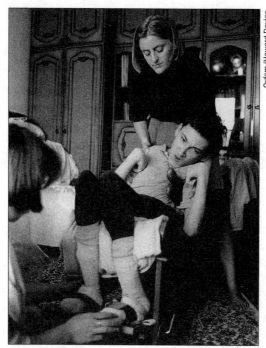

Oxfam/Howard Davies

left Physiotherapists Barbara Jennings-Jayaram and Azra Begtasagovic on a home visit to Mirza Musafendic in 1996. Home for Mirza is a top-floor flat in a high-rise building, with lifts that are frequently out of action.

medical resources of the State, followed in order of priority by war-injured civilians; people who had been disabled before the war were mainly neglected by over-stretched medical services dealing with more urgent needs. Wheelchair-users living in the typical high-rise blocks in modern Bosnian towns were trapped when electricity supplies were cut, leaving lifts inoperable. People with hearing impairments could not hear the siren that warned of shelling, and 17 people were reported killed in Tuzla alone because they were unable to run for shelter. For all those with sensory impairments, obtaining information became increasingly difficult, and their support system — whether the State welfare system, neighbourly support, or their families — disintegrated.

Disability allowance was no longer paid regularly, and amounted to only a few pounds a month when it was paid. Many disabled people found it impossible to attend distributions of humanitarian aid — either because they could not see or hear the information about where distributions were happening, or because they could not physically travel there. Some disabled people have needs for special items apart from any specific medical needs: anti-decubitus cushions and moisturising creams for wheelchair-users, for example. Clothing with very small buttons and shoes with difficult-to-tie laces also posed problems for some disabled and elderly people. When asked, disabled people are very clear about specific needs: more changes of thermal underwear for people with limited mobility — who are more susceptible to the cold — incontinence pads or nappies, slip-on shoes and clothing that is easy to fasten. It used to be true that the special needs of particular groups were rarely taken into consideration in emergencies. This is slowly beginning to change, but undoubtedly the fittest and most able will always be able to get access to support systems much more easily than the people who most need support. When food resources are limited, the fittest get priority; when a mother has to flee with her children, there is little chance that she will be able to help her disabled relatives too. Many disabled people were confused by the lack of information, left behind because of their limited mobility, forgotten by aid agencies, and even (it was alleged to me by several people whom I interviewed for this book) deliberately targeted for attacks — at least after Operation Storm, when the Croatian army retook the 'Krajina' area and displaced about 200,000 Croatian Serbs into Bosnia.

The institutionalised system of care

Before the war, rehabilitation services for disabled people were based on residential institutions. Medical rehabilitation was usually carried out in hospitals or clinics in either Croatia or Serbia. Once medical rehabilitation was finished (at the point when the medical professionals decided that nothing further could be done to improve the physical condition of the individual), the next move was either back home, or to an institution.

In Yugoslavia there had been a network of residential institutions, for adults and children, each specialising in a particular impairment. There is a divergence of views on institutions, with a clear split between the experiences of people with less-disabling impairments and the experiences of the most severely disabled people. Some institutions seem to be well-respected, and there is little sign of the kind of abuse which has been exposed in some residential homes in the UK. Whether abuse on any scale occurred or not is hard to judge. In fact, many people with less severe impairments initially speak with warmth and gratitude about their time spent at various institutions in Former Yugoslavia. However, when questioned at length, some relatives of severely disabled children speak about neglect and mistreatment in the institutional system, which they felt powerless to challenge. It is the most severely disabled people who are most at risk of abuse or neglect, and there is no independent system of monitoring or protection. There is also an emerging anger and frustration among less severely disabled adults, as they learn more about different systems in other countries and realise that it was not strictly necessary for them to have spent their childhood away from their families and in the care of impersonal strangers. The international presence in Bosnia has played a large part in creating an awareness of other options in terms of social support systems.

Caring for a severely disabled child on a daily basis puts immense pressure on other family members — especially primary carers, who are usually mothers — but now families can see other options, such as day-care centres, and overwhelmingly want their children to live at home with them. The children themselves are frightened by the thought of having to leave their parents: after all, no child would ever choose to leave the security of his or her family to live in an institution with over a hundred other 'cases'. Parents of children who would have been sent to institutions before the war are now struggling to care for their children at home, and to fight for places at kindergartens and special schools. Both children and parents are reluctant to go back to the centralised institutional approach.

Unfortunately, little has been set up to fill the gap that has been left by the institutions which have been destroyed or closed, are now on the 'other side', or are being used as refugee centres. During the war, families who were already under intense pressure, coping with daily needs such as collecting water and finding food, were not able to offer the support which their disabled children needed to develop and grow. Some disabled children have attended regular schools as an emergency measure during the war, but as the situation improves they are likely to be incorporated into efforts to rebuild the old system. Indeed, there are plans to build a number of new institutions which are large, usually isolated from the community, and impairment-orientated (an institution for the blind, an institution for the deaf, an institution for people born with cerebral palsy, for example). As international reconstruction funds pour into Bosnia, the government hopes to obtain finance to rebuild institutions. Very few of the donor agencies have social-policy advisers for reconstruction projects or seriously consult social-development agencies.

An opportunity for change

However, some of the emergency measures adopted during the war now offer hope for a different future for disabled children. Ironically, the destruction of the old system offers a great opportunity for change. The influx of international agencies from a wide variety of countries also gives a great opportunity for comparisons and for learning about the successes and failures of models from other countries. As Nermina Corhodzic, the mother of a child at the Koraci Nade Centre, told me:

> ❧ It's ironic that during the war nowhere would accept my child and I had to resort to travelling to this centre. I didn't think it would be as good as an institution, and it worked in a strange way. In the old system we never saw any progress, but now I can see much more improvement in her condition. She can do much more, and she's happier. Now I can see other possibilities for her in the future. Isn't it strange that it took this awful war for us to get a centre like this? ❧

A system of associations and unions of disabled people was very well established before the war; some had been in existence for over 50 years. They were funded by the State through the Bosnian national lottery and had a large membership, but worked within a very bureaucratic system, with power generally centralised in the capital. When war broke out in Bosnia, the lottery collapsed and — just when their membership needed them most — the associations were facing a crisis. During the war their role quickly became the provision of urgently needed relief supplies to their members, contacting aid agencies and government logistics centres which distributed relief. Some associations were established during the war solely in response to the needs of their membership. Disabled people, inevitably isolated, were the hardest target group for aid agencies to reach, but the associations which did have the means to reach individuals were rendered ineffective by lack of funding and resources.

Later in the war and during the post-war period, only the Association for Disabled War Veterans has received government funding. Other associations are trying to re-establish pre-war income-generation activities, such as photocopying services, shoe-repair workshops, and small-scale production. However, their role as non-government agencies is unclear, for their relationship with the State has always been close and they were not completely independent.

There are considerable numbers of disabled people who are not represented by any association. Women typically play a minor role in these bodies, and some groups have yet to develop a democratic process which will guarantee a system of genuine representation and accountability.

Oxfam in Bosnia

Oxfam (UK and Ireland) first began working in Tuzla, an industrial town in the north-east of Bosnia, in 1993. Tuzla was surrounded on three sides by active front lines, and its pre-war population had risen dramatically as refugees fled from Serb-controlled areas. For much of the war there was only one road out of Tuzla, which involved skilled driving over a dangerous mountain track in a four-wheel drive vehicle, carrying bullet-proof jackets and helmets.

Oxfam also has offices in neighbouring Serbia and Croatia. Until late 1995 the Belgrade office implemented work in Serbia and Montenegro, as well as in the eastern enclaves of Bosnia, which could be accessed only through Serbia. The Zagreb office carried out programmes in Croatia, including the Serb-controlled areas of Croatia, as well as functioning as a regional office.

The signing of the Dayton Peace Agreement in November 1995 made many areas much more accessible, and aid agencies were able to operate in areas where it had been virtually impossible before. Just a year after the Dayton Agreement, Oxfam had opened five offices in Bosnia, in addition to the Tuzla office. New programmes were begun in Gorazde, Livno, Bijeljina, and Banja Luka; and the regional office has been moved to the Bosnian capital, Sarajevo.

Initially the Oxfam programme focused on the supply of winter clothing and shoes to virtually all sections of the population, but especially to displaced people living in collective centres. The winter of 1993/94 was extremely cold and dangerous for the people of Tuzla; many were at risk of simply freezing to death. Later on, work began on a development programme, to complement the purely relief-orientated programme. But the provision of relief remains a crucial part of Oxfam's work in Bosnia. Despite the improving general situation, there are still large numbers of very vulnerable people. Oxfam operates a considerable programme of support for women, either directly or through local organisations, which especially focuses on displaced women and deals with issues of missing family members, women's rights, income generation, and skills training. The economic situation is not, of course, a subject of concern solely for women, and Oxfam's support in this area is also directed at small producers and disabled people.

Oxfam's approach to work in conflict is based on the conviction that affected communities are most likely to cope with and recover from the traumatic events of war if they are helped to regain control over their lives and livelihoods, taking action for themselves, and rebuilding the social and community networks which offer support in difficult times. While self-help approaches take responsibility away from the State, which should provide essential services for its citizens, the reality is that during wartime most people have to rely on their own resources in order to survive.

Oxfam's approach to long-term development stresses the need for a unified programme, incorporating advocacy and campaigning work, particularly to promote the basic rights of marginalised people; the development of a strong and independent non-government sector; and support for the efforts of community groups to challenge and influence a government not meeting its obligations. Guarantees of human rights, justice, and redress are, of course, central to any community's recovery from war.

The social model of disability

Disabled people, including children, have rights. Oxfam promotes the 'social model' approach to disability, which, rather than obliging individual disabled people to change and adapt to an inaccessible society, aims to make society accessible to disabled people. Peter Coleridge, in his book *Disability, Liberation, and Development* (published by Oxfam in 1993), broadly outlines the social model of disability: '*The social model of disability begins from the point that integration is ultimately about removing barriers, not "normalisation", cure, or care. Rehabilitation within a comprehensive social framework is about the removal of barriers at the individual level; it is also about the removal of physical and attitudinal barriers in society at large.*' The social model is essentially an approach and an attitude, rather than a prescriptive list of actions and interventions.

The Oxfam team in Tuzla has developed a whole range of complementary projects and actions which all play a part in the promotion of the social model. So the Koraci Nade Centre, which is the focus of this case study, is intrinsically linked to other projects, such as the Lotos Resource Centre for disabled adults and the ZID workshop for the production of enabling aids for disabled people.

A 'social model' approach also incorporates support for the development of associations of disabled people, and attempts to incorporate a disability focus into projects with women, collaboration with local NGOs, and relief distributions (with varying degrees of success).

This approach depends on disabled people taking a prominent and active role in project design, decision making, and project management. It sees far beyond the specific impairment of the individual, and deals with the social, economic, cultural, legal, and political dimensions of disability. Human rights are central to this approach: the right to an education, to employment, to health care, to play and develop as a child, to protection from violence and abuse, to political participation, to nourishment and water, and, most fundamentally, to life itself. The social model requires disabled people themselves to define the services they require, and promotes the idea of an inclusive society.

Although the two approaches are not mutually exclusive, the 'social model' approach is commonly perceived as an alternative to the 'medical' or 'individual' model, which focuses on the individual and his or her specific impairment, which is perceived to be in need of 'correction'. In the medical approach the individual is seen as the source of the problem, not the environment in which that person lives. The medical model tries to change the individual to fit into society, rather than promoting social change to enable all citizens to be active participants. Institutions are a result of the medical approach, and they focus primarily on the medical needs of disabled people rather than human rights, education, employment, and accessibility of the environment.

A project with disabled children, approached from a medical model, may offer nothing more than medical services. Without doubt, this is necessary: children all over the world are denied access to essential health care and medical services, and disabled children may have specific medical needs because of their impairments. But the 'social model' approach goes further. It concerns itself with promoting the rights of disabled children, does research on national legislation and policies which define their situation, and helps them to confront social prejudice, besides campaigning to improve their health-care services and to establish their right to appropriate medical care. The project may provide medical services, but as part of an integrated approach which sees the whole child in his or her environment, instead of focusing on his or her impairment(s). It will try to address the roots of the child's problems, which often stem from prejudice and barriers both architectural and institutional.

However, by simply taking on the role of the State and the community in providing for the essential needs of disabled children, or by encouraging disabled people to begin 'self-help' projects, development agencies can actually make the situation worse. A balance has to be achieved between providing essential services as an immediate and urgent intervention and taking away responsibility from local authorities or national governments for meeting the needs of their populations. The next chapters look in detail at the Koraci Nade Centre and Oxfam's efforts to meet the urgent needs of a group of severely disabled children in the short term and its current attempt to transfer the Centre, and its radically different approach to disability, to the State system in Bosnia.

Oxfam/Howard Davies

above *'Doctors with white coats in cold rooms frighten the children. Here they get physiotherapy surrounded by toys, laughter, and their friends'*: Azra Begtasagovic working at the Koraci Nade Centre with Sefik Hamzic, 16 years old, who was born with microcephalus.

Koraci Nade: Steps of Hope   2

First steps towards a disability programme

In March 1994 Tuzla field staff, with support from Helen Lee, Oxfam's UK-based Disability Adviser, who was visiting the field office, began the process of promoting disability as an integral part of Oxfam's work in the area.

Oxfam has a theoretical commitment to disability in its programmes all over the world, but actual work on disability issues has not been done in a strategic or considered way: the promotion of disability issues depends very much on the initiative of field staff and regional managers. If staff feel unsure about the issues, they obviously need support and resources. The Gender and Development Unit had been promoting gender issues within Oxfam, both in its internal systems and in field work, publishing a wide range of literature and resources, and supported by the fact that UN agencies and other international organisations were also putting gender, at least in theory, high on their own agendas. Disability, however, did not have the same status as an issue for a number of reasons: the deep-rooted prejudice in most societies and cultures about disability; the segregation of people with disabilities, which meant that many staff had no direct contact with disabled people; the perception of disability as a medical/clinical issue rather than a human-rights concern; and the significant lack of disabled staff members within development organisations.

When the Eastern Europe and Former Soviet Union (EE/FSU) department was set up in Oxfam in 1992, in response to the disintegration of social services in these areas, there was a real opportunity to ensure that disability was on the agenda right from the start. Although there were UK-based and overseas staff skilled and experienced in implementing disability-aware programmes, the EE/FSU desk was the first department to have its own Disability Adviser, working solely to increase awareness, train staff, develop resources, and collaborate with UK and global networks. The post of Disability Adviser was later discontinued, partly through lack of funding and partly because it was judged that sufficient skills had been transferred to local staff; but it had clearly played an essential role in promoting disability, and raising the awareness and confidence of field staff in beginning work with disabled people.

The Disability Adviser made her first visit to Tuzla in March 1994, inspiring field staff to begin an initiative that was loosely termed the 'disability unit' in the field office. Although this was not a 'unit' as such with a mandate and clear aims, it was seen as a catalyst for promoting an awareness of disability in Oxfam's programmes in the area. Two field staff were charged with initiating work with disabled people: the Deputy Country Representative and an interpreter who later became the Tuzla Programme Coordinator. The Disability Adviser, on a visit to Bosnia, began to train these two staff members in disability issues and met with disabled individuals and associations representing disabled people in the area.

The initial needs expressed by disabled people dictated the approach which Oxfam was to develop. A number of pre-war disability associations had tried to continue to meet and represent their members, but the war played havoc with their attempts: there were no telephone lines, lack of transport was a constant problem, the shelling of the town made it unwise to be outdoors, and they had absolutely no funding. Their main problem was the enormous need for material assistance for their members, especially food, clothing, medicines, and enabling aids such as wheelchairs and hearing aids. Again and again these needs were expressed by disabled people, either through organisations representing them, or by the individuals with whom Oxfam staff had made personal contact. Prejudice and discrimination, inequality and isolation were mentioned as long-term concerns, but survival on a day-to-day basis clearly took priority at this time.

However, it was these very barriers — social and physical — that made the day-to-day survival of disabled people so difficult. In the short term, Oxfam was able to provide clothing and footwear and enabling aids, while planning for longer-term interventions to improve the situation of disabled people. The prevailing emphasis of work was on building a close relationship with associations of disabled people. This was a difficult and time-consuming task, but the links established at this time provided the foundations for much of Oxfam Tuzla's subsequent work with disabled people. One of the problems in establishing a relationship with the associations was that their main concern was getting humanitarian aid, a need that Oxfam sometimes was able to meet and sometimes not. Interest in future work on organisational development, basic rights, and advocacy too often depended on how many relief parcels Oxfam could provide to meet urgent and immediate needs.

Another role for Oxfam staff was advocacy on behalf of disabled people during the daily briefing sessions with other international agencies, and to ensure the widest possible dissemination of information among disabled people in the community. At the same time, the field office was preoccupied with trying to find premises accessible to wheelchairs — not very easy in the valley town of Tuzla, where only two buildings (the old people's home and the main hotel) had ramps.

Links with the Association of Women

One major problem was simply finding information about disability. Very few books on the subject were available in the local language. Alma Subic, one of the first two staff members in Tuzla to be trained by the Disability Adviser, recalls:

> ❝ We wanted to find out some more information about disability, but not from a clinical point of view. So Helen suggested that we just ask some women, as they always know about these things. And that's how we met the Association of Women. I think that Oxfam's interest in gender also led us to talk to women, rather than the male-dominated associations of disabled people. The Association of Women was the only women's organisation at that time, although there are lots now. ❞

The association's main aim was 'to promote equality for women in all spheres of life'. However, its president, Ajsa Mahmugtagic, was also a teacher for young people with learning disabilities, and had set up a support group for mothers of disabled children living in collective centres. The feedback from mothers involved in the group had been very positive, and the association had asked if Oxfam would be willing to support further development of this work.

Oxfam staff immediately began to follow up this lead, but found that there was a marked difference in approach between themselves and the Association of Women. While Oxfam wanted to support a small grassroots project, the association made a proposal for a large centre with many staff, very ambitious aims, and a big budget. In discussions with the mothers, who were the primary carers of disabled children, it was clear that they were desperate for some kind of support for their children. In the weeks of consultation that followed, the mothers began to define their needs specifically as being able to take their children somewhere safe while they attended to their daily business (collecting aid parcels, visits to the various government departments, shopping, and caring for the other members of their families) and being able to get together with other mothers to form a support group. But this would be much more than a child-care service: the mothers wanted professionally qualified people to be caring for their children and providing services for their education and development.

Oxfam began to make more and more direct contact with the mothers, and finally realised that the project must go ahead regardless of whether agreement could be reached with the Association of Women about the size and approach of a possible centre. A small budget was found as part of the funds for a broader UNHCR-funded rehabilitation programme. A room was rented, a few toys provided, and the Support Centre for Disabled Children and their Mothers opened on 25 June 1994.

Early days at the Support Centre

The Centre opened as an Oxfam operational project — with Oxfam retaining direct managerial control — rather than providing funding to the Association of Women to implement and manage the centre as a partner organisation. The staff were recruited from the Association of Women, in order to keep the links and retain the possibility of handing over management to the association in the future. The Association of Women were very disappointed by Oxfam's decision to go ahead with a project that had essentially been their idea. Oxfam staff felt that the approaches of the two organisations were essentially in conflict with each other, but expectations had been raised among the mothers, and the only option was to go ahead independently.

Cimeta Hatibovic was the first co-ordinator of the project and had actually written the original proposal from the Association of Women. She describes the first few days when she was trying to locate the disabled children in Tuzla. At this time one of the main problems was the heavy shelling of the town, which made all movements very difficult and dangerous.

❛ I went to the Centre for Social Work and asked for a list of all the children in the various categories. I went through every document from the past four years, to get hold of some addresses so that we could contact parents and children about the centre. Then I went to the hospital for neurological treatment and did the same, but I hardly got any information. I also went to the health centre and Kreka Rehabilitation Unit. In the health centres they were so busy with the wounded that they had no time to help me. It was the same story at Kreka too: the doctors and nurses were so busy that it was really difficult to get information. Finally at the paediatric clinic at the hospital they had all the names, but no addresses; for some there was just the name and then 'Tuzla' as the address. I didn't know what to do. I had all the names and there were a lot of children, but I didn't know how to contact them. Next I went to the MZ ['mjesto zajednice': local council] and went through the register to find each individual address. I had to go to the MZ for each area. Once I had the addresses, I had another problem: no telephone, no post, no transport. So I explained what we were doing to all the MZ staff and gave them details about the Centre and asked them to pass the message on to anyone they came across. Then I had to go back to all the other places to leave the same information. All this time Tuzla was being heavily shelled.

Soon after that, some parents got in touch with me and on 25 June we had the first meeting with the mothers. The next day we started work with the children. The first day there were ten children, but each day more and more came. We worked just four hours each day in the morning. The parents started telling other parents about the Centre, and we also went out trying to find families with disabled children. We looked everywhere we could and explained what the Centre was doing. For example, one day I saw a woman in the street carrying her child and I just went over and asked her about the child and told her about the Centre. After that she came every day. The girl has cerebral palsy and her mother didn't know that she also had sight problems; we found out about her sight and helped her with some exercises for balance, and now she is attending the school for blind children. ❼

Very soon practical needs became apparent: a carpet, a few musical instruments, some modelling clay. However, none of these things could be bought in Tuzla: despite the end of the blockade, the only goods being brought into the town were food items. The nearest place to buy such items was in the port of Split in neighbouring Croatia, which served as a logistics base for aid agencies and UNPROFOR operations in Bosnia. However, depending on the weather, the drive to Split could take between 10 and 48 hours, at least half of it off-road. International agencies travelled together in convoys of two or more vehicles, and frequent accidents made the road impassable. So progress was slow and delays were plenty.

Initially the mothers enjoyed the chance to do essential tasks — which had been difficult before, due to the lack of transport and the restricted mobility of their children — and the opportunity to socialise with each other. Some mothers spent more time with their children than others; some pushed their children harder and were more willing to work on their children's development. Gathering together meant that the more active mothers helped to inspire the others to work more directly with their children. At this time there was no end to the war in sight, and the children needed immediate attention; there was no possibility of local or government authorities investing in the project.

Problems of staffing and funding

Many professionals who had been working with disabled children and adults had left Bosnia during the war, and those who stayed were mobilised into military or civil service. Some found that they could earn more money working for aid agencies as interpreters and drivers than in their chosen profession. The mothers were particularly concerned about the development of speech, but there was only one speech-therapist left in Tuzla. A physiotherapist was also needed, but getting access to health-care professionals who were in such demand everywhere was very difficult.

The lack of long-term planning for the project had left it with minimal financial support and no long-term strategy, which, according to Alma Subic, who later became Oxfam's Programme Co-ordinator, was a source of many of the later problems:

> ❛ The project didn't really have any thought or direction — it just seemed to happen along the way. At the beginning there were no funds allocated to it, and that was a huge problem. In retrospect I know we should have planned it a lot better and should have defined clear aims and objectives and identified a funding source — that would have saved us a lot of problems. It used to cost us 1,400 Deutschmarks a month [about £600] for rent, staff, equipment, everything. It was really a miracle that the project survived. I was supposed to be working just as an interpreter at the time and I didn't even have a contract with Oxfam when the Centre opened. ❜

Despite the initial uncertainty and confusion, within six weeks of the opening clear plans for the development of the Centre were being drawn up. Many children who wanted to attend the Centre were not able to do so for lack of transport: either there was no regular public transport from their homes, or it was inaccessible to them because of a mobility impairment. So the first plan was to buy a vehicle, so that some sort of taxi service could be set up. A vehicle would also allow staff to visit children in their homes: an outreach component would mean that those children who were most isolated or marginalised could be reached.

The office staff responsible for the project were developing a clear idea of Oxfam's approach to disability, of the rights for disabled children, and how to promote the 'social model' as opposed to the medical model. However, the staff employed in the Centre had been trained and worked for many years as part of a system where the medical model of disability was ingrained. The promotion of the social model as an alternative way of looking at disability needed someone familiar with this approach to work on a day-to-day basis with the staff, parents, and children in the Centre. If this person was a medical professional, he or she would have the status needed in order to work on an equal basis with Bosnian therapists. The Centre desperately needed further physiotherapy inputs, and it was decided to recruit for one year an expatriate physiotherapist who was familiar with the social model; but the recruitment of a person with the appropriate skills proved to be very slow, partly because of the prevailing war-time conditions.

Meanwhile, the Centre had expanded its working hours and taken on more staff, although it was difficult to find professional therapists who were not already obliged to work in Tuzla's hospitals or with military wounded. Sometimes finding staff was the result of a lucky coincidence. Azra Begtasagovic came to the office because she heard that Oxfam had been carrying out a shoe distribution. The distribution was actually happening at the Support Centre, so Oxfam staff gave her a lift and found out on the way that she was a physiotherapist whose work-place had closed down during the war. She began work at the Centre the next day. A speech-therapist, Nevzeta, was recruited; no speech-therapy services were available in Tuzla at that time, and the Support Centre became the only place where severely disabled children could improve their communications skills. A psychologist also started to work in the Centre at the request of the staff and parents.

By the end of the year the enormous need for the project to continue and take on more children was obvious. The staff were afraid to publicise the work of the Centre, because they simply could not cope with any more children. In January 1995 Oxfam obtained funding from the Overseas Development Administration (ODA) of the British government: £50,000 for disability work, which included £25,000 for the Centre for 1995, as well as costs for a physiotherapist to carry out training in the Centre. In March 1995 a UK physiotherapist with overseas experience in community-based rehabilitation and promotion of the social model of disability arrived in Tuzla and immediately began work in the Centre.

The early part of 1995 was a difficult time for Oxfam in Bosnia. The Country Representative, who had arrived in October 1994 and had just begun to train the Tuzla team in equal opportunities, was seriously injured in a car accident in January and was unable to return to Bosnia until April. New staff had been recruited to continue the work initiated by the Disability Adviser and the Deputy Country Representative; they were eager to push forward the disability work, but needed time to become familiar with the project, with Oxfam as an organisation, and with the Bosnian environment. On top of this, in late March the winter cease-fire abruptly ended as a spring offensive started and Tuzla again came under regular shelling.

However, it was also an optimistic time for the project, as Cimeta Hatibovic told me:

> ❰ When I heard that the physiotherapist was coming, I felt great, because it seemed that Oxfam was really committed to the Centre. It was very good when she came, because we didn't have enough professionals able to work in the Centre because of the war, and Azra needed some support. When she arrived, we all felt a lot more enthusiastic and had much more incentive. It was about that time that things really started to get going. ❱

This extra professional support helped the Centre staff to organise a better routine, putting children into groups, organising different sessions at set times, and developing an administration system with individual documentation of all children and their progress. A work-plan was drawn up each week, and team meetings were held, to plan future work and developments within the Centre. The outreach component also began to get going, and a

above Barbara Jennings-Jayaram and Azra Begtasagovic working with Senka Selmanovic on a home visit in 1996.

34

vehicle was bought to enable the staff to visit children who could not come into the Centre for any reason. The UK physiotherapist also worked intensively on further training with Azra Begtasagovic, who remembers the early days and the later changes that were initiated at this time:

❟ In the beginning we had just a few children, and I was trying to work more socially rather than just as a physiotherapist. I was very lucky, because Cimeta is very experienced and she shared her knowledge and skills with me. At the beginning there were just the three of us working here and trying to get the Centre established, but there were big problems with shelling and transport. Soon we bought the Lada and more children started coming. In fact the Centre was growing every day. When the shelling got really bad, we were forbidden from opening the Centre by the local authorities, so we started the outreach. When we were working with a particular child, it was very important to see where that child lived, to see the family relationships and the social setting. In the beginning I was just doing the typical therapy we had learned, mainly massage, but when the physiotherapist came, she showed us some other ways of working. Before we had always worked separately and individually with each child, but she introduced group working, and we saw much better results in the children's development.

One example is Martina, whose mother had been to Slovenia and Croatia, to some special institutions, to try and get help for her daughter. The mother learned all the exercises very carefully, but actually there wasn't much improvement. What Martina really needed was the stimulation of being with other children. She had problems sleeping and going to the toilet, and was really scared of other children. Her mother had taken her to a famous institution for cerebral palsy in Zagreb, and when she was there she started to have more problems than before, especially as she was alone at night. Finally her mother took her away from that institution. Once she started coming to the Centre and mixing with other children, she started to progress almost immediately — the group-work approach that the physiotherapist introduced really worked much better than individual work. Children need to be with other children. The doctors with white coats in cold rooms frighten the children. Here they get physiotherapy surrounded by toys, laughter, and their friends. When we play some games, especially ball games, all the staff, the children and the mothers play together; it's fun and it's relaxing too. Before there were only institutions; now children can get some help near to their homes, and their parents can be involved too. ❟

So a physiotherapist with experience of working in a very different environment was able gradually to introduce a new approach. Because the training took place on a daily basis for a long period of time, the staff were able to see the results, and were not tempted to slip back into their former methods as soon as the trainer had gone. There was some resistance among the staff team to the new approach, because it contradicted much of what they had learned, but two and a half years later the same staff members are enthusiastic about the new way of working and are training others to adopt it.

However, there were some problems. The level of training for a physiotherapist in the UK is much higher than in Bosnia, and the UK consultant's skills and experience were consistently under-rated by the Bosnian professionals whom she encountered, particularly because Bosnian physiotherapists do not make a diagnosis or treatment plan. It also meant that the Bosnian physiotherapists with whom the consultant was working were less knowledgeable about their profession than she had expected.

Originally the idea of having a non-Bosnian physiotherapist had come from discussions with the Director of the Kosta Popov School for Children with Learning Difficulties; the staff of the Kreka Rehabilitation Unit were also very keen on the idea. However, poor communications and the already heavy demands of the Support Centre meant that the UK physiotherapist was unable to work in the other two institutions. Changes in personnel meant that new staff in Oxfam were unaware of previous commitments that had been made. The result was that both Kosta Popov School and Kreka Hospital were disappointed and disillusioned with Oxfam. The UK physiotherapist was keen to focus on training, so that she could leave skills behind, rather than doing hands-on work which could only act as a short-term stop-gap; but the fact that non-therapists had planned the terms of reference for the physiotherapist post meant that the workload had been over-estimated. Unfortunately the misunderstandings with these two institutions created a tension which lasted for much of 1995 and 1996. The problems which Oxfam is now facing as a result of its poor relationship with representatives of local authorities and the State system are described in more detail in Chapter 5.

Is integration between disabled and non-disabled children possible?

The majority of children attending the Support Centre had learning disabilities, cerebral palsy, Down's Syndrome, or a sensory or mobility impairment, but non-disabled children from another Oxfam centre in the same building sometimes joined in. The Art and Music Centre next door specifically targeted displaced children from three large collective centres in the neighbourhood. From the beginning the location was seen as ideal, because it would allow joint activities between disabled and non-disabled children. However, prejudice about disability formed a much bigger and stronger wall than the one which separated the two centres, and it proved very difficult to develop one integrated centre from two very separate ones.

In the Art and Music Centre there were already problems of aggression between displaced and local children. Local children and staff felt that the displaced children, who were mainly from rural areas, lacked social skills. Already overwhelmed by conflict between local and displaced children within the Centre, and by Oxfam's attempts to make them confront their own prejudices, the staff felt unable to cope with a programme of integration with disabled children as well. In dealing with prejudice there is often a naive assumption that simply explaining the facts or holding a training workshop will somehow lift the veil from people's eyes, and prejudice will suddenly disappear. A long-term approach was needed to identify and deal with prejudice, but there simply was not enough time, as funding had almost run out for the Art and Music Centre and no further funds would be available unless it was merged with another project. The legacy of running two centres which essentially segregated disabled and non-disabled children was that any natural process of integration had been stifled. Inadvertently Oxfam had contributed to the notion that disabled children should be separated from non-disabled children.

The professional staff working in the Support Centre were convinced that only qualified professionals were able to work with children, especially children who had been displaced because of the war. At the time there were many 'psycho-social' projects in Bosnia, and 'war trauma' and post-traumatic stress disorder were considered to be endemic. All the Bosnian people had been affected by the war to a lesser or greater extent, but Oxfam's policy was not to run clinical psycho-social projects, or to assume that people who had suffered very distressing experiences would necessarily become mentally ill. Instead Oxfam chose to work on facilitating the rebuilding of community structures and supporting traditional coping strategies. However, the emphasis on professionalism in Bosnia and the number of trauma-orientated clinical projects had given rise to a general feeling that anyone working with people in war-time had to be a qualified professional in a recognised discipline such as psychology, or defectology in the case of disabled children. Yet Oxfam had chosen young students who were creative and musical to work in the Art and Music Centre. Part of the reason was practical: simply that the students were available. But another reason was to break away from the idea that children's centres had to be run by psychologists or other professionals, and that displaced children were so traumatised by their experiences that they needed clinical intervention. For those children who did need specialist professional help, there was a whole range of projects run by other agencies to which they could be referred for assistance.

Oxfam's commitment to employing non-professional helpers in the Art and Music Centre did not diminish the prejudice of the professional staff in the Support Centre. Conversely, the helpers in the Art and Music Centre were prejudiced against the disabled children next door. Rural/urban prejudice is common in Bosnia: often disabled people in villages were considered to be products of inter-marriage or general 'backwardness'. The prejudice against rural people among the urban elite is very strong, and endorsed by the value accorded to professional qualifications (rural people being very under-represented in higher education). All these factors were at work and played a role in blocking the process of integration. The relationship between the staff running each of the centres began to deteriorate rapidly. Some of the problematic issues are illustrated by the opinions of the co-ordinators of the two centres.

Elsad Bijedic, co-ordinator of the children's Art and Music Centre at the time, explains the problem as seen from the point of view of his staff:

> ❢ The way that we tried to integrate the centres wasn't necessarily wrong, but the major problem was the people. You need people with an open mind. We tried integration with refugee kids from the villages, but they don't know anything about disability; kids from the towns have more culture. The point is that disabled kids in the villages are different. In the villages the problem is superstition; in the towns there are more medical services and more correct information. Refugees have to solve their own problems first, before they can start to look at the problems of disability. ❢

And Cimeta Hatibovic explains the situation from point of view of the Support Centre staff:

> ❢ In the beginning there were two centres next to each other, but the idea of integration between the centres didn't work very well, because the normal children didn't want to mix with handicapped children. The Support Centre didn't have very good premises or resources, and refugee children didn't want to come. There was also a problem with their staff: they didn't like the idea of integration, because it meant putting effort into trying to change the children's attitude about disability.

There were already problems in the children's centre, because the staff didn't know anything about psychotherapy, for example, and they weren't professionals — they didn't know how to work with children. The idea of integration wasn't so good, because it involved trying to change years of a system overnight. Later we had training [in conflict-resolution and team-building] with Alex [Jones, a trainer who later became Oxfam's Deputy Regional Representative for Former Yugoslavia]. That was fantastic: she brought us something really new — a very progressive approach. We were relaxed and laughing. After the training we took the mothers out to a restaurant for lunch — that was wonderful, really effective. **7**

These two points of view illustrate not only the prejudices within each staff team, but also some of the fundamental problems which faced Oxfam field staff in trying to bring the two centres together. Whereas the staff of both centres were unwilling to be open-minded about integration, Elsad Bijedic does highlight a key problem: integration cannot be achieved without preliminary work within the community to counter the negative attitudes that are engendered by the medical approach. This point was reinforced by Alma Subic, who was responsible for trying to bring the two centres together:

⌊ We tried to impose integration without creating the pre-conditions for it to work; we tried to force integration where there was no natural process. First we have to work on our own awareness of disability; for example, we should work with schools. Now that the centre has activities that are interesting for both disabled and non-disabled children, it is more successful and more natural. **7**

So the staff in both centres felt that integration was being forced upon them. They did not know how to adapt their activities to allow for disabled and non-disabled children to play together; and they were unwilling to face up to their own prejudices. Perhaps this was inevitable, given the project's ambitious aims and lack of resources to carry out those aims. The professional staff in the Support Centre had no respect for the young students running the Art and Music Centre; equally, the staff in the Art and Music Centre resented the professionals and felt that they were always treated as amateurs.

When the time and resources are not available to spend on addressing prejudice, it is a hard choice to keep on staff whose attitudes are at odds with their organisation's approach and working principles. Should the organisation concentrate on working through issues with existing employees, or risk discontinuity by recruiting replacement staff with more sympathetic attitudes? As funding ran out for the Art and Music Centre in August 1995, Oxfam decided to restructure both the centres, which had been so close together but had operated completely separately. The idea was to have one centre for all children, which would provide special support for disabled children. In this one centre there would be a restructured staff team, reflecting the way in which the new centre would work. There would be group workers who would carry out group activities with children, aiming to stimulate their development in an enjoyable way; these activities would be suitable for both disabled and non-disabled children.

Oxfam also decided that it was not appropriate to have a psychologist working at the centre. Each of the mothers caring for a severely disabled child was under considerable stress, and some children were suffering from sleeplessness, fears, and nightmares; but if a child was frightened when a shell landed close by, this reaction seemed, from a common-sense point of view, a rational and normal response, rather than a sign of a traumatic stress disorder. As mental-health interventions were not an activity in which Oxfam felt confident and knowledgeable, it was decided to leave this area of work to other, more experienced, agencies in Tuzla. The Support Centre closed down for a week; recruitment was carried out for posts in the new structure; and the Koraci Nade (Steps of Hope) Children's Centre opened in September 1995. The new name was chosen by a group of children and parents to reflect how the Centre represented their hopes for the future.

An integrated centre

The staff of the new Koraci Nade Centre were also sceptical about possibilities of integration. There were no examples of integrated projects, and their education as defectologists had been based on a very separatist model. Oxfam's insistence on trying to integrate the projects was at times stressful for the staff, who felt that they were being expected to achieve the impossible and even something that was fundamentally wrong. Moreover, the parents did not want their non-disabled children mixing with disabled children, because they thought it would slow down their development. When the parents of disabled children added their voices, saying that the more mobile and physically active non-disabled children disrupted the centre and made fun of the disabled children, it really did seem an impossible situation. However, foreign staff knew from their own experience in other countries that it *was* possible, and they persevered in working towards an integrated centre.

Gradually it began to work. Fata Ibralic, a defectologist employed as a group worker, explains:

❮ At first it was difficult for me to accept Oxfam's approach. When I was training as a defectologist, we had a separate professional for each impairment, and it was very difficult for me to work with children of such mixed abilities and age groups. But after 13 months of working in the Centre, I can see that the children learn much better from each other. Initially there were some problems with the non-disabled children, with prejudice and fear, but after a while they just naturally started to play together. This Centre is trying to achieve something very ambitious and is the first step towards an integrated approach to disability in Bosnia. Maybe the fact that students of defectology are coming to the Centre for working practice will mean that in the future Bosnia will see a whole new approach in practice. The Faculty of Defectology is very interested in the Centre; you can see this because they send their students here: they like Oxfam's approach. ❯

Fata's job is to design games and play activities, mainly for the children with learning difficulties, which will incorporate the exercises they need to stimulate their further development. She describes how the centre works on a daily basis and how this new approach has changed her view of her profession as a defectologist:

❮ After my initial bad experiences of trying to work in this new way, we started to get the Centre much more organised, and I started to use the new techniques like the group work. One problem was that we never knew which children were coming when, and we didn't have their details, so we started to keep records and make our own assessments. For the children with the most severe learning difficulties, those considered to have a mental age of less than two years, I assessed their development in terms of communications, socialisation, self-help — that is their ability to get dressed, washing, going to the toilet, eating and so on — and their interest in their environment. The activities for these children were based on that assessment. For children who had been categorised as having a mental age of between two and four years, I assessed them on the same principle: self-help, communications, socialisation, and work — the ability to carry out a task or activity. We made charts for each child and coloured in their progress in a different colour every six months. This way both the child and the parents can see the progress the child has made. The group activities were games that helped the children to practise their speech, and moving their arms and legs, balance and co-ordination, and their awareness of their own body.

The children enjoy the games very much. Most of the children in the centre need help in all these areas, so we get into a group and all practise together. The children who cannot exercise on their own have another staff member or a parent supporting them. We also have a daily programme of art, plasticine work, dancing, music, and so on for each child. I am really happy when I see the children progress, and when they don't want to go home because they enjoy the Centre so much.

We never worked like this before the war. You can only work like this if you really love kids. You have to have your heart in your job. I feel as though I am pushing past the limits into something new. I am really happy in my job as a group worker, learning so many new things and seeing our progress towards integration. Students of defectology never learned about this kind of approach until now. In the Faculty I am an assistant in three of the subjects for mental retardation, clinical treatment for mental retardation, and pre-school mentally retarded children. I have just started a pre-school component here. It was the first day yesterday and some students are coming from the Faculty to see the pre-school class. Each class has five or six disabled children and two or three non-disabled children. This is the only place where students can come and learn about working with severely mentally retarded children. This is the only centre of its type in Bosnia. **7**

Oxfam/Howard Davies

above Koraci Nade Centre, Tuzla: '*When we play games, all the staff, the children and the mothers play together; it's fun and it's relaxing too*' (Azra Begtasagovic).

Oxfam/Howard Davies

above The ZID workshop: Azra Begtasagovic works with Denis Jusufi, Sead Korabegovic, and Muhamed Selimovic to construct a seating unit for a child at the Koraci Nade Centre.

The ZID workshop

Another initiative during this period was the training done by a worker from the British charity, Motivation. Motivation have assisted people all over the world to set up workshops to produce, adapt, and repair wheelchairs, using low technology. Each workshop is run by disabled people themselves. The trainer's original brief was to carry out wheelchair mobility training and investigate the possibility of a sustainable wheelchair workshop in Bosnia. Without doubt this would be a difficult task, with the supply of materials, tools, and equipment a major problem in a country at war. The first visit was postponed a number of times because of security problems and doubts about what could actually be achieved in the difficult circumstances. Soon after the trainer's arrival in October 1995, the pressing need for seating units for many of the children with cerebral palsy at the Support Centre was identified, and the trainees in wheelchair repair soon began to turn their hand to the design of seating units. Five volunteers, all themselves disabled, started to work in a makeshift workshop which had previously been used by the children's Art and Music Centre.

Azra Begtasagovic, the Koraci Nade physiotherapist, describes this part of the disability programme:

❦ Many of the children desperately needed aids, so we started up the workshop. Now it's called ZID [Zivot Ide Dalje — 'Life Goes On' in English]. Before the war they just handed out standard wheelchairs, but it's important that the chair or seat is specially designed for each individual child — or it can actually make the child's condition worse. When ZID opened it was great; it provides a lot of aids for the kids. For example Natasha is eight years old and has severe problems with cerebral palsy: she has very poor head control and muscle contractions in her hands, and she also has problems with her legs. She is a tall girl and growing quickly, and her mother is finding it more and more difficult to help her. Natasha often had to wait until her father came home from work. Now ZID have made a chair for her which supports her head and holds her body in the correct anatomical position in order to improve her posture. She really enjoys having the chair; it has made so much difference to her life and she can go out with her mother now. **'**

By November 1995 the Koraci Nade Centre had started to work in a much more organised manner, the outreach component was well-developed, and the ZID workshop was just beginning to produce essential enabling aids and exploring the potential for future expansion. It had been a difficult year. Tuzla had come under regular shelling; one attack, on 25 May, left 71 young people dead, killed by a single shell — an incident which left the whole town in shock. In July the towns of Srebrenica and Zepa had fallen to the Bosnian Serb Army, with the ensuing displacement of almost 35,000 people — mainly women and children — into Tuzla. When an October cease-fire was agreed, it brought a welcome break from the hostilities, and the peace negotiations were coming close to making *this* cease-fire a permanent one.

Peace and reconstruction 3

A lasting peace in Bosnia?

In November 1995 the Bosnian Peace Agreement was signed in Dayton, Ohio. Despite uncertainties about whether all parties would cooperate, finally the Presidents of Croatia, Bosnia, and Serbia signed the agreement. The Dayton Agreement, while trying to promote a multi-ethnic Bosnia, in fact formalised a partition of the Reppublika Srpska and the Muslim-Croat Federation areas which broadly followed the front lines as they stood.

In Bosnia the reaction to the peace agreement was one of scepticism: after countless cease-fires, people needed to see real change on the ground before they could have faith in the Dayton Agreement. A cease-fire agreement in October had already stopped the shelling, but winter cease-fires were a regular event, because of the severe cold and inhospitable terrain. If the peace could last beyond the spring, when the new offensives usually began, that would differentiate this agreement from all the others.

In fact other changes brought about by the cease-fire began the following month. US troops were deployed as part of the Implementation Force (IFOR) which had replaced the UN Protection Force (UNPROFOR). Tuzla airbase was host to 20,000 US troops, who trundled into Bosnia in green tanks and wearing army fatigues, in contrast to the white vehicles and blue berets of the UN Peacekeepers. The US troops entered Bosnia from Croatia to the north on a route which they intended to be opened to civilian traffic. This road, dubbed Route Arizona by the US military (who renamed every route in their area after a town or state in the USA), was the former main road north to Croatia and Hungary which had crossed three front lines during the war. Using this road it was possible to travel to the Croatian capital, Zagreb, in four hours, rather than risking the arduous three-day journey on rough and dangerous roads which had been used for most of the war.

Aid agencies were encouraged to use this route, albeit with care because of the mine fields that flanked much of the road, in order to build trust among the Bosnian citizens. All sides were wary of passing through what had been 'enemy territory'. But soon this road became a commercial bus route, and then a route for civilian cars as confidence grew. Most importantly, the opening up of Route Arizona allowed commercial traffic to enter Bosnia again, and the shops started to fill with new goods. A large market opened on the route to Tuzla; it was a meeting place for people from the two sides who met up with friends and family whom they had not seen for three years or more, and travel between the entities increased as confidence in the peace agreement grew. Suddenly Bosnia started to feel like part of the real world again; goods from Western Europe were on sale; commercial businesses started to multiply; and the army checkpoints that had thwarted all efforts to travel from one town to another without prior police permission were gone.

The town of Tuzla changed from being the end of the line after a long exhausting journey to a stop-off on the route from southern Bosnia to Croatia, Hungary, and Austria in the north. Although the US troops were mainly confined to their bases and travelled through the town in convoys of four vehicles, a 'Dayton Café' opened, then an 'American Club', and the US flag started to appear at roadside bars run by Bosnian entrepreneurs, hoping to take advantage of the wealth of their new guests.

But this is not to say that there were no problems, or that more than a year after the Dayton Agreement there is trust and confidence between the former warring parties. Justice is a crucial precondition for future peace, but the War Crimes Tribunal has, for various reasons, been unable to try many cases of alleged atrocities. Nor have the persecutions and discrimination of minority groups stopped; but there is, at least, a feeling of hope for the future.

A time of transition for aid agencies

For aid agencies, the changes brought about by the Dayton Agreement allowed not only an unprecedented freedom of movement, but also a chance to re-assess their priorities. Just days after the peace agreement, most agencies were already engrossed in analysis of what the future would hold for Bosnia, planning where to allocate resources, and predicting who would still need assistance in the future. The general situation in Bosnia was undoubtedly improving, but large numbers of people were still displaced within Bosnia or abroad. A massive reconstruction programme would have to begin on a nation-wide scale. Freedom of movement for civilians was still problematic in towns such as Gorazde, which was, in effect, still an enclave.

For the Oxfam Tuzla team it was a difficult time of transition, trying to keep up with the rapid changes in Bosnia, and all too aware that the peace might not last. In effect, they were planning for optimism and sustainable peace, while also making more pessimistic contingency plans for renewed military action in any area, or for a political or terrorist crisis. During the months following Dayton, a number of minor crises did occur, but massive international pressure managed to keep Bosnia reasonably stable.

An evolving role for the Koraci Nade Centre

During this period the Koraci Nade Centre continued to develop in the new atmosphere of hope for the future. The Lada still provided essential transport for staff and children, but increasingly it spent time off the road being repaired, as a little more mileage was squeezed out of it. The Centre continued to focus on the family-based approach, and the staff worked as a team to ensure that each family had regular visits, despite the transport problems. This was especially important for the more isolated families, and those children with the most severe impairments who could not use public transport. Improved administrative procedures contributed to better organisation and smoother running of the Centre.

As the only centre of its type in Bosnia, Koraci Nade attracted much attention from other agencies who were able to offer support. They included the Italian government agency, Cooperazione Italiana, which paid for a group of disabled and non-disabled children and their parents to visit the Croatian coast in the summer of 1996. This was the first time that most of the children had seen the sea, and for many of the parents the first visit outside Tuzla since the start of the war, as the Croatian coast had been inaccessible for four years. Like the restaurant meal for mothers during a training session the previous year, the seaside holiday had a tremendous effect on morale for staff, children, and parents alike. In fact, one young girl who overcame her fear of water by watching other children play in the sea, and then joining them, still talks endlessly about the joys of swimming.

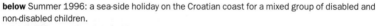

below Summer 1996: a sea-side holiday on the Croatian coast for a mixed group of disabled and non-disabled children.

Oxfam/Howard Davies

47

However, as hopes for long-term peace increased, and the conditions in Tuzla slowly improved, the physical faults within the Centre became even more apparent. The premises were poorly equipped and furnished; the toilet was appalling — awkward even for the most physically able people, never mind the children with mobility problems — and funding was still a concern. The premises were available only a short-term lease, so Oxfam was reluctant to invest too much capital in the building.

At this time a proposal was being drafted for several of the disability projects under the umbrella of 'Rehabilitation Services'. The Rehabilitation Services proposal was for £100,000 to fund the Koraci Nade Centre, the ZID workshop, and further training, including an extension to the physiotherapist's contract to enable her to work with the project staff for a further four months. It also included a new minibus to enable more of the severely disabled children to get to the Centre, and a budget for equipment and training which Oxfam hoped would enable responsibility for the Centre to be transferred to local authorities. The proposal was accepted by the UK Overseas Development Administration, which guaranteed a further year's survival for the project, and time to identify a permanent solution for the centre.

The ZID workshop continued to produce enabling aids for the children in its makeshift premises, and in May 1996 finally moved into a building which had been renovated by Oxfam and already housed the Lotos Resource Centre for disabled adults. Even though they were now physically separated from Koraci Nade, the ZID technicians worked very closely with the Centre, producing aids which enabled the children to take a more active role in their communities. Denis Jusufi, a rehabilitation technician in the ZID workshop, explains:

> ❦ We see Azra very often; we talk on the phone every day and go on home visits on Tuesdays and Thursdays to see the children. Mainly we carry out small adaptations to wheelchairs and make seating units for the children. We have a close link to the Centre and support it very much. I know that parents of non-disabled children are hostile to the idea of integration, but it's a new idea and we will keep trying, because people are always sceptical about new ideas until they prove themselves. ❦

Azra Begtasagovic related the story of one young girl, Fikreta, whom we went to visit, along with Denis and Ferid from ZID, in her village about 90 minutes' drive from Tuzla:

> ❦ Fikreta is 7 years old and has cerebral palsy. She lives in a village quite far from Tuzla. She's never walked, but can write with her left hand,

although she's very slow. In terms of her mental abilities, she is very bright, but if she goes to a special school she will have to follow the curriculum for mentally retarded children. Her local school didn't want to accept her; the director just didn't want her going there, because she can't walk. He said that he cannot have her in his school, and that he has no legal obligation to take her. Anyway, her mother came and talked to us, and we told her that her daughter does have the right to go to school, and after a small battle with the school director she has now been going to school for 15 days, but she also comes into the Centre for some special support. Before, her mother used to carry her two kilometres up a muddy hill track, so that they could get the bus and come to the centre. We are planning to go and talk to her teachers to see how things are going. So far, Fikreta is the only child who cannot walk who is going to regular school. **⁊**

The day we visited Fikreta, Denis and Ferid from the ZID workshop brought her a new seating unit for a follow-up fitting. After her 15 days in school, Fikreta had made lots of new friends and the director of the school had apologised to the family for trying to obstruct their attempts to get her into school. So, while Fikreta and her family will no doubt have many future battles with the authorities, they at least have the support of Koraci Nade and ZID, and her experience can give hope to other disabled children that they also will be able to go to school one day.

Another group which is supporting disabled children and their families is the Association of Mothers of Disabled Children. The association grew out of the Association of Women, but is actually a separate group. It was begun by mothers of disabled children who were dissatisfied with the lack of support they had received from Koraci Nade. Staff from the Association of Mothers are just beginning to work with the Koraci Nade Centre and accompany staff on their outreach visits.

New funding priorities in peacetime

Following the Dayton Agreement, other parts of Bosnia became increasingly accessible, and needs in these areas were apparent. As Oxfam began programmes in Banja Luka, Gorazde, and Bijeljina, resources began to be transferred from the Tuzla office to the new programmes. Vehicles, computers, communications equipment, and core funds were transferred to other locations, yet the Tuzla programme was still the same size. The needs in other parts of Bosnia, especially eastern Bosnia in the Republika Srpska, were immense and bordered on life-threatening. While everyone recognised the priority of working in these areas, continuing commitments in Tuzla area meant that a fine balance had to be maintained.

The movement towards long-term sustainability in the Tuzla programme had begun at the end of 1994, when the UNHCR-funded women's rehabilitation programme had been the first to take the plunge and develop from an Oxfam operational project into a local NGO. Given the lack of independent local NGOs in Bosnia, all Oxfam's projects up to this point had been operational, rather than implemented through a local partner organisation. Most other international NGOs were working in the same manner and the Bosnian government had just started to draft legislation to regulate the registration and operation of local NGOs.

The women's rehabilitation programme registered as BOSFAM (Bosnian Family) in November 1994, but it was still very dependent on Oxfam for warehousing, logistical support, reporting and accounting, and looked to Oxfam, as its main funder, for direction and guidance. With a year, however, BOSFAM was functioning as an independent NGO, obtaining funding from other sources as well as Oxfam, and very much steering its own development. The Tuzla office hoped that other operational programmes would follow the example of BOSFAM where appropriate, thus ensuring the most efficient use of Oxfam's resources.

The decision to scale down operations in Tuzla and to expand operations in other areas assumed that the programme was geared solely to meeting immediate needs, and that it could be transferred to other areas as needs changed. But the Tuzla was more than an emergency-relief operation. It had begun to analyse the factors which marginalised its target groups, and was developing long-term projects to help them to address the problems and bring about real change. By transferring resources immediately, the three years of work in Tuzla would have collapsed when the programme was very close to reaching a point of reasonable sustainability. But acute needs in other parts of Bosnia needed immediate action too, and the budget would stretch only so far.

This was one of the key concerns expressed by the Tuzla Programme Co-ordinator, Alma Subic:

> ❟ Oxfam has long-term projects, and must show a long-term commitment to them. Oxford [Oxfam Head Office in the UK] sometimes has far too high expectations and puts a lot of pressure on field management staff for projects to become sustainable when the conditions for that don't exist. Because there was no long-term commitment, everyone was afraid of losing their jobs and in general a

feeling of uncertainty and insecurity existed. Lack of planning in the initial stages caused many problems. We all had short-term contracts. Staff would change, and each new staff member would have their own ideas and visions of the project. It should have been the other way round — the project having clear objectives and each new staff member just continuing the work of the previous one, in line with the aims. **⁊**

Although this 'short-termism' clearly had a detrimental effect on staff morale, and little long-term planning was achieved, it is arguable whether long-term planning would have been possible in the circumstances. The security situation meant that international staff could have been evacuated, the programme could have been frozen, and communications cut off at any time. To issue long-term contracts or make long-term plans for projects at that point would have gone against the prevailing priority in Bosnia, which was day-to-day survival. In any case, Oxfam Tuzla was simply not able to make that commitment: it could not guarantee that the projects would continue; everything depended on external circumstances which were unpredictable and uncontrollable. What was possible, however, was scenario planning, whereby the staff team and project staff looked at a number of possible scenarios, including an immediate peace agreement, an escalation of fighting and evacuation of civilians, or just a continuation of the *status quo*. By considering the different possible scenarios and their possible outcomes, it was possible to talk honestly with staff and others involved in Oxfam projects about what they could expect from the organisation in each circumstance. We return to this issue in Chapter 7, which looks in detail at the realities of working in conflict.

For a project to be able to exist without the presence of the implementing organisation, it would need to be completely self-sustaining in terms of funds, equipment, transport, materials, skills, and so on. Many Oxfam operational projects were beginning to reach this point, but they still needed some support, especially in terms of funding, bank accounts, and financial management. Representatives of donor agencies were now more able to travel in Bosnia to visit projects in person than they had been during the conflict, and they were more discerning about funding priorities. Although this improved the direct dialogue between donors and implementing staff in the field, it was difficult to achieve a balance between meeting the donor's criteria, following the implementing organisation's own policy, and providing what the actual service users wanted. The Overseas Development Administration (ODA) of the British government has continued to provide crucial funds for the Koraci Nade project and Oxfam's other disability work in Bosnia. ODA representatives have visited the project a number of times and have been very supportive in recognising that projects like Koraci Nade take time for results to show. The same representative, visiting in 1995 and 1996, was able to see a great improvement in the Centre, and enabled the staff to recognise just how much they had achieved in that period. An open and honest dialogue between donor and implementing agency is crucial for long-term planning and learning on both sides.

However, as Bosnia lost its prominence in the international media, its share of aid budgets began to shrink. While high-profile emergency work is relatively easy to finance, it is harder to raise funds to deal with the long-term effects. Most aid agencies were being funded from the emergency budgets of various international donors and donations from the public, who rely on media coverage for their information about situations in far-off parts of the world. Core costs such as staff salaries, vehicle maintenance, office and warehousing space, international telephone and fax lines, and so on are an essential part of any operation, but notoriously difficult to fund.

Concern about continued funding of the Koraci Nade project put pressure on all the staff, who were aware that each year a new proposal was put to a donor for repeat funding and that results were sometimes hard to see. There was certainly pressure to make all projects independent and sustainable. A large number of projects registered as local NGOs and were able to get very substantial funding from international and UN donors, who prioritised local organisations. Unfortunately one of the negative effects of this policy, as seen in many other parts of the world also, is that large sums of money are given to organisations which have not had time to develop the managerial skills and organisational structure to achieve their aims effectively. There is a general tendency in these cases to respond to the donor's agenda, rather than to develop skills in assessing the needs of target groups and communicating with them.

A sustainable future for Koraci Nade?

It was in this context that planning for the future of Koraci Nade began. There was no doubt that the Centre was meeting urgent social and medical needs — at least half of the children attending the Centre still have no other option — and that the project needed to develop into a long-term service. Parents were very clear on this subject: there is literally nowhere else for them to go, and they are very worried that the Centre will close. Every parent who contributed to this casebook has emphasised, some with great desperation, the need for the Centre to continue. Yet the Tuzla team and the project staff had to take a step back and look at the situation from a less emotive viewpoint, in order to plan for real sustainability.

The national and regional government structures were moving out of the crisis phase that had left many departments unable to meet their obligations during much of the war. Government plans were emerging for a reconstruction of the pre-war system, for larger and more modern institutions. Several were planned for Tuzla, and an 'expert group' proposal to meet the needs of disabled children focused on size and type of building, rather than the type of care. Overwhelmingly international and local agencies working in social development opposed the government plan, and several heated debates were held. The depth of misunderstanding between this 'expert group' and international agencies was illustrated when a tentative agreement was reached that 'mini-institutions' would be a good way forward. Defining what was meant by a 'mini-institution', the Norwegian representative who made the proposal was visualising centres in the community with up to four children and live-in carers — yet it emerged that the 'expert group' was thinking in terms of between 60 and 100 children accommodated in one 'mini-institution'!

Oxfam wanted the Koraci Nade Centre to continue in some form, the priority being that all the children should continue to receive at least the same level of care and support in the future. But the project could not continue as an operational project for ever, and nor could funds be raised indefinitely. There were two options, which had been outlined in the original proposal in 1994: either to become a local NGO, or to become part of the government system. The staff themselves favoured becoming an NGO. Many people working for local NGOs had considerable freedom in their work, were paid well, and had good resources and facilities, owing to the policy of major donors such as UNHCR (the United High Commissioner for Refugees) to focus on the funding of local NGOs. Those who continued to work for the State were in a less certain situation in the short term, even though the local NGO sector was still very donor-led and was unsustainable without international donors. For government employees, salaries were low and sometimes not paid at all; there were no funds to pay the running costs of existing services, let alone a new centre; and few resources were available from State funds.

Moreover, the staff in the Centre began increasingly to define its aims, visualising for it a much broader role in bringing about social change than it would have as a State-sponsored service. Azra Begtasagovic defined the aims of the Centre as follows:

> ❢ Firstly, the education of parents and the whole family to enable them to help their children more; secondly, improving the children's social skills; thirdly, improving the functional adaptation of the children so that they can do everything they need to, for example go to the toilet etc.,

as much as is possible for each child; fourthly, to support the parents and give them a break from their children; and finally, to work on the education of teachers, parents, and children in ordinary schools to make a integration a reality. **▼**

Links with the Kosta Popov School

It was in the months following the Dayton Agreement that the future of the Koraci Nade Centre was mapped out. Not only was the State system being revised, but other agencies with a focus on developmental and rehabilitation projects were beginning to appear on the scene. Through its advocacy work, Oxfam had come to be associated with disability issues, and new agencies coming into the area were frequently referred to Oxfam. These were agencies whose programmes were primarily focused on social development; but Oxfam had gone further and was trying to influence reconstruction agencies to improve physical access for disabled people, and was also trying to promote debate about the wisdom of reconstructing institutions. Oxfam and similar organisations hoped to develop a dialogue with reconstruction agencies, to persuade them to work in partnership with social-development agencies and seek their advice on the social implications of their projects. The aim was to preserve and develop the community-based structure which had emerged as the former centralised system broke down during the war. The most pessimistic prediction was that the former system of impairment-specific, separatist institutions would simply be rebuilt; the most optimistic ideal was that reconstruction funds could be used to influence the development of community-based services which focused on the basic rights of disabled people and their integration into society. The most realistic option lay somewhere in between the two.

In November 1995 the Italian Red Cross arrived in Tuzla to assess the possibilities for reconstruction projects for children, beginning with a request from the Municipality of Tuzla to build an extension to the Kosta Popov School for children with learning disabilities. The proposal primarily involved building a dormitory block so that 200 children could become residents of the school. The same proposal had actually been submitted to Oxfam the previous year, and Oxfam and the Koraci Nade Centre had links with the Kosta Popov School.

The Kosta Popov School, the largest of its kind in Bosnia, accepted children from all over the region with mild to moderate learning disabilities. About 270 children attended during the pre-war period; those from farther afield were accommodated with local families during the week, the families receiving an allowance to cover extra expenses. When the war started, ten of the 28 teaching staff left for Serbia or Serb-controlled parts of Bosnia, and transport problems and lack of incentives for host families meant that attendance dropped to 160 children, attending the school during the mornings only. Staff and children were arriving at school hungry and cold, and there were very few basic school materials. The school also has a number of occupational workshops for adult graduates from the school, but these had run out of materials and were barely functional.

Oxfam had been supporting the school from 1994 with distributions of shoes and clothing for staff and children, and materials for the workshop, and was a frequent customer of its printing workshop. However, co-operation with the school was not always easy: Bosnian guidelines on the teaching of children with learning difficulties restricted Oxfam's attempts to promote the social model of disability. Negotiations were begun for Oxfam to recruit a physiotherapist to work as a trainer at the school, but additions were made to the terms of reference to cover work with the Koraci Nade Centre and the outreach project, and when the physiotherapist was finally recruited and arrived in Bosnia, she began to work mainly with the Koraci Nade Centre. The school was not happy with this situation.

By the time Oxfam and the Italian Red Cross had made contact, the directorate of the Kosta Popov School were feeling very negative about Oxfam and unwilling to co-operate. However the Italian Red Cross delegate, Andrea Placidi, was very interested in consulting Oxfam, not only about the social implications of extending an institution and therefore the promotion of institutional care, but also about the specific aspects of designing a building for disabled people. After months of trying to influence those who were implementing re/construction projects, Oxfam was eager to take this opportunity.

At the same time, the Koraci Nade Centre had been told that it had to move from the existing premises, and the staff were desperately scouting around buildings in Tuzla to try to find somewhere central and accessible. Finally one building was located — a former kindergarten at a local factory — but it needed extensive renovation work. While a proposal for renovation funding was being written, a restaurant gained permission to use the building, and the search began all over again.

At the same time, Oxfam was increasing its co-operation with the Italian Red Cross and helping them to define the details of the construction project. Andrea Placidi recalls:

> ❡ We approached Oxfam as part of a number of visits to agencies working in the same field, and we were also recommended to come to Oxfam by UNHCR. The project would probably have been very different

if we hadn't spoken to Oxfam first and been to visit the Koraci Nade
Centre. The Centre influenced us a lot, especially in terms of the need
for physical adaptations such as ramps. During those first few weeks we
decided to go ahead with the Kosta Popov project, because the school
already existed, and both Oxfam and Cooperazione Italiana with their
different projects would be there to offer support and advice. Oxfam had
already prepared the ground for a different approach to disability and
could give support during the process. The Red Cross always looks at the
social and community implications of a construction project, but Oxfam
was helpful in defining the exact details. The support was great. We saw
a gradual change in the project as we visited the Centre, visited the
school, and began to get a clear idea of the needs of the children. For
example, we realised the need to incorporate a social area as well as the
original request for dormitory space. In terms of physical accessibility,
this project is an ideal example, because it was designed for accessibility
from the very beginning. It is a project for disabled children, though,
and other agencies working on other types of project don't think about
the access problem. **𝟕**

After many hours of discussion with Oxfam, the Italian Red Cross finally drew
up a proposal for the extension of the school, including a plan for a social
centre. Oxfam was opposed to creating a residential institution, especially as
many of the children attending the school had mild learning disabilities and
there was no reason for them to live in a residential institution when facilities
for educational support could easily be provided in their community.
However, it was clear that at some point the project would go ahead and that
the Italian Red Cross shared a vision of a more flexible approach and an
opening up of the institution.

With no alternative premises available for the Koraci Nade Centre, Oxfam
started to see that the socialisation area within the Kosta Popov School extension
could be a solution, if the local authorities would give their agreement. However,
while the various local authorities had become more positive about the Koraci
Nade Centre and its approach, some were still hostile towards Oxfam, and wary of
taking on additional responsibilities while they were still in financial crisis.

A report by Oxfam field staff points out one of the main problems of the
planned move to the Kosta Popov School:

❹ Oxfam has started negotiations with the local authorities for the
Children's Centre [Koraci Nade Centre] to become part of the existing
social services structure. These negotiations have indicated the results

of Oxfam's work in Bosnia-Hercegovina, as the authorities have been very positive about the social model of disability, which was not the case in 1993, when Oxfam just started to work in this area. The main problem with this plan is that the local authorities are wary of taking responsibility for the centre, as they cannot guarantee running costs of existing services, never mind take on new obligations.

Oxfam has worked in close co-operation with the Italian Red Cross, which started the project of building the dormitory for Kosta Popov School. In this building there is a large socialisation area which could be used for the Children's Centre. The school directorate, Italian Red Cross, and Oxfam are keen for the centre to become legally part of either the school or the Faculty of Defectology, but both are worried about the financial implications of taking over the centre. While Oxfam does not wish to create parallel social services, and it is clearly the role of the local authorities to provide such essential services for its citizens, the issue of running costs will be difficult to resolve. **⁊**

So back to funding problems again. However, one plan did emerge to overcome the problem of who should take financial responsibility, and who should take managerial control. If Oxfam could pay the entire running costs for a set period, and then gradually reduce its input as the local authorities became more and more able to cover costs, the Centre would at least have a chance to continue for another year, when the situation could be very different. By making a financial contribution, Oxfam would also retain some influence over the future of the new Centre, for example by being represented on a management board, or by paying staff costs on the condition that the Koraci Nade staff were kept on in the new Centre. This would avoid making anyone redundant and ensure that staff trained in the 'alternative' approach were running the new centre.

The report continues:

❟ Oxfam finds the idea of the Centre becoming part of the existing structure very interesting and a good way of pushing things forward. We will be looking for possible donors for the Centre for the coming period. This idea is very attractive, as the Centre will be in a better position to influence positive changes in the Kosta Popov School, where the social model of disability still has to penetrate, and to push for the integration of the disabled into the community with special emphasis on education as the starting point for integration. **⁊**

The transfer of the Koraci Nade Centre to the Kosta Popov School has the potential to influence change in the institution. The Centre could become a route for channelling children with mild learning difficulties out of the institution into mainstream schools, and carry out training with teachers, parents, and children to prepare the ground for gradual integration in schooling. Moreover, by training staff to deal with children who have severe physical as well as intellectual impairments, it would become possible for those children for whom there are currently no services to attend the institution, which would have a much stronger relationship with the community. The possibilities of such a move are great, but the problems of funding, management control, Bosnian legal restrictions on the education of disabled children, and Oxfam's poor relationship with some local authorities will have to be overcome.

The politics of disability and 'democratic' elections

According to the Dayton Peace Agreement, elections were to be carried out in Bosnia before 15 September 1996. The time-frame was very tight for a country still divided along ethnic lines and recovering from war. However, during the summer of 1996 political activity became more and more obvious, with posters, campaign meetings, and the flags of political parties flying at every cross-roads. The Organisation for Security and Co-operation in Europe (OSCE) was given the onerous task of supervising the electoral process — its most ambitious task to date.

In 1991 Bosnia had held its first multi-party elections, which had played a crucial role in exacerbating nationalist tensions in the run-up to the war. The 1996 elections in Bosnia were a first step towards creating a post-war democratic political structure. As such they could have presented an opportunity for local NGOs and lobbying groups to raise issues with politicians in open meetings. But most Bosnians were not used to approaching government and forcing it to be accountable to the people; it would have been a most unfamiliar and uncomfortable role for them. The majority of the political parties, and certainly the largest and most influential ones, followed a nationalist agenda which played on the insecurity of the peace in Bosnia. Women's groups managed to promote concerns such as the large number of missing people, especially from Srebrenica, but service provision for disabled children did not have the same status and public support as an issue. The opportunity to use elections to raise issues with the government was missed the first time round, but there is an increasing awareness that groups of parents can be powerful, and organisations such as the Association of Mothers have played a central role in politicising parents in the Koraci Nade Centre.

I spoke with Njaz Zulcic, a parent at the Koraci Nade Centre, about the role of parents in lobbying the State to meet the needs of disabled children. He first told me the story of his experiences during the war, and then of his expectations and hopes for the future of his daughter, Amela. The Zulcic family are originally from Bijeljina in the Republika Srpska, about an hour's drive from Tuzla on the far side of the Majevice Hills, which formed the front line for much of the war and were the scene of heavy fighting.

▌ Amela had a hard time during the war. Before, we had everything we wanted — a house, a garden. She wasn't living in an institution. She had just been in Belgrade for eight months for speech therapy — apart from that, she lived at home. We lived in Bijeljina, and in January 1993 we were forced to leave our home by the Serbian authorities, so we went to stay in the house of a friend who had already left because of the war. By August 1994 they were collecting non-Serbs off the streets and 5,000 people came from Bijeljina into Tuzla. But we stayed. We hid inside the house for a year and a half — it was just like being in jail. All the non-Serbs they collected on the streets were sent to the front lines to dig trenches. In terms of food there wasn't a supply problem as there was in Tuzla; it was just difficult to go out. There was a lot of flour and big devaluations of the currency: in the morning a loaf of bread would cost one DEM, and by evening you could get nine loaves for one DEM. It was my wife who went out to get food — it was too dangerous for me. Luckily the house we were in had a big wall around the garden, so Amela and I were able to go into the garden sometimes, but mostly we were inside.

When we finally were forced to leave for Tuzla, we were two days on the road and sleeping outside beside the road. Amela was used to being inside mostly, so it was difficult for her. By the time we got to Tuzla, she was so scared that she just refused to go out. She is still scared of shells and she remembers where they landed — every one she remembers, exactly where it landed. She understands why we had to leave Bijeljina, she knows that we were forced out.

When we first arrived in Tuzla, we were in the students' hall, which was a collective centre for refugees; but my wife has a sister here and we went to live with her very soon after arriving. Later we found our own place. We just have the same problems as other refugees; the problem is that there are so many of us here. We managed to bring some money and some jewellery and here we get humanitarian aid like all the others. We don't work — all the firms are closed down. We will go back to Bijeljina one day. My wife and her sister have been back four times and I plan to visit there; a friend of ours has already returned and hasn't had any problems. In Bijeljina our apartment was owned by the local authorities, but a woman from the Ministry of Education came with the police because she wanted our flat, and we had just ten minutes to leave. The Dayton Agreement says I can go back to my flat now. We will see: maybe there will be another war here in Bosnia.

I don't know what the future will hold for Amela. It will probably be like before the war — it will be her family giving her support. Even here she doesn't get enough, she just comes to the Centre. We heard about the Centre about five months after we had been here. When there was too much shelling we just stayed at home, but some of the staff came to our place to see us. It was very hard for them and dangerous, so they just came three times. Disabled children need support, and this Centre is excellent for bringing children together and for them to play. Here in the Centre the children have choice — they are not forced to do something they don't want to. Amela was very closed before and she didn't communicate very much.

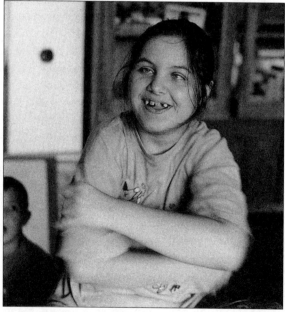

above Amela Zulcic at the Koraci Nade Centre. Her father comments: '*Amela was very closed before and she didn't communicate much. After she started coming here, she really progressed. At the weekends she just waits until Monday when she can come here again; she loves it, and it is having lots of positive benefits in her life.*'

After she started coming here, actually in a very short time, she really progressed. At the weekends she just waits until Monday when she can come here again; she loves it and it is having lots of positive benefits in her life.

It would be great if this centre could become part of local services. This country needs lots of centres like this — our taxes should pay for it. We cannot ignore the needs of disabled children — they are part of society too. Whatever happens, the Centre will continue. Even if they try to close it, the parents will take over. We will somehow get the money to keep it running. We need everything to help our children grow and develop and learn — it doesn't matter who gives it to us. Most of the parents don't have any money to pay for services; they will accept everything that is available. We will fight to keep the Oxfam Centre. I pay my taxes so that we can have Centres like this — Amela has the same rights as any other child. Before the war, the country paid for everything, but we only had good services in the big cities. I often had to take Amela to a hospital or clinic in Belgrade so she could get some speech therapy. Now I pay my taxes to the Bosnian government, so I expect the Bosnian government to take responsibility for these children. We have to fight for the rights of our children — if we don't fight, no one else will. I am a member of the Association of Mothers* and will have a strong voice, and someone will have to hear it!

Now we don't really know what the future holds. Our government is concerned with other problems, and our problems are at the bottom of the government's priorities. We must fight and make sure they know about our problems. After all, when you go to the doctor they can't start to help you until you've told them what your problems are, can they? We will fight together with our friends, and Oxfam is one of our friends.

In Bosnia we cannot ask too much. Our elections are not even close to what you have in the UK or USA. You have democratic elections; we just had one party before. You have candidates who will do everything you demand; we don't even have that here. Maybe in ten or twelve years, maybe. Now we are in the post-war period; we have to recover from the war. We need time, because our mentality is different from yours: we just look straight ahead and don't see the sides. That's why we have all these nationalist parties. ❜

[*The Association of Mothers of Handicapped Children was founded by a group of mothers, but does not exclude fathers. The name reflects the fact that many more mothers than fathers are primary carers for disabled children.]

During the post-war period the Koraci Nade Centre bloomed in the development of its administration and working practices. The difficulties experienced by the staff in adapting to a new approach were in the past, and they were now actively promoting the social model in their work. While funding continued to be a concern, the ODA Rehabilitation Services grant at least covered the Centre until March 1997. After that, the future is uncertain. The Italian Red Cross extension to the Kosta Popov School should be finished in spring 1997, but there has been no definite confirmation that the Koraci Nade Centre will be able to move to the school. At the time of writing, negotiations are continuing to explore ways of managing the Centre, the level of funding which Oxfam would be able to provide for running costs, and how Koraci Nade's radical approach would fit into a State-controlled structure. On the positive side, the parents are very keen for the Centre to continue in its present form (but with a better physical environment), and are willing to organise themselves to support the move to being part of the State system. While the idea of the lobbying power of community groups is new in Bosnia, there is very strong feeling on this issue, and the parents may well be the key to negotiating a sustainable future for the Centre, and appropriate service-provision for their children.

Tackling institutional prejudice 4

Any development-agency project will reflect the organisation's internal structure, policy, and working practices. It is therefore essential that the internal ethos of the institution is consistent with the intended outcome of the project in the community. Development agencies approaching disability from the perspective of the social model need to look critically at their own practice — in recruitment, in equality of opportunity, in policy and advocacy, in support for groups of disabled people, in consultation, participation, and representation in their staff teams, as well as in project implementation. Whereas these agencies may have a special unit, team, or working group to monitor policy and practice, an approach based on the social model should be central to all aspects of the organisation's work. Using the experience of Oxfam's team in Tuzla, this chapter looks at the problems involved in trying to change attitudes within an organisation as a prerequisite for managing effective projects that will promote a change of attitudes in society.

Dealing with prejudice and discrimination is one of the most crucial factors in an effective approach to disability. In society it is attitudinal barriers that disable: negative attitudes of town planners, architects, designers, service-providers, and so on create architectural and institutional barriers. Within a relief and development agency, the commitment of the staff team is crucial for a project's success. Attitudinal barriers can do immeasurable damage to any attempts to work on an equal basis with disabled people. Yet all individual staff members within an organisation will, to a varying extent, be affected by the prevailing attitudes and beliefs of their society, and will share its particular forms of prejudice and discrimination.

An example of how difficult it can be to change attitudes within an organisation is the work that has been done on gender within Oxfam. Oxfam has a gender policy and a team of people working specifically on the issue. There are also a number of manuals and texts available to support field workers, published both by Oxfam and by other organisations. Gender issues have a high priority in many UN agencies, which means that field staff are often working in an environment where concern about gender equality is shared by counterparts and partners. Despite this, and the resources invested and the valuable achievements of the Oxfam Gender and Development Unit, the adoption of a gender-fair policy has not been without its problems in Oxfam. This is especially so at the field level, where a broad organisational gender policy has to take into account many different cultures and beliefs. One would think that, because gender-fairness is an issue for all people, it is more likely to be of interest than disability, for example, which is perceived as directly affecting a smaller group of people. In fact, it is surprising how frequently the term 'gender' is misunderstood, and how it is possible to work within an organisation which has an overt focus on gender without really addressing gender issues at all. Oxfam, as yet, has no disability policy, and its concern for the issue is expressed only sporadically. In those areas where field staff have taken the initiative to work on disability issues, and where support has been available (for example from the Disability Adviser for Eastern Europe), considerable change has taken place. But, at an organisation-wide level, given the attention and resources that have been put into work on gender, and the problems that remain, the possibility of addressing disability issues in the near future without further input and resources is very limited.

The participation process

One of the principal concerns and frustrations of most disabled people is that their services are in the main controlled by non-disabled people. Yet, if disabled people are among the poorest and most powerless people in the world, then all development projects should be 'disability-aware', and therefore disabled people should be active participants in any development project.

In development work the participation process itself is crucial to achieving the end result. Many projects have been found not to have achieved their planned results; but, although they might seem to have failed in some respects, they have had many positive effects along the way. For example, there are many ways to try to influence or change government policy. One way is to support a community group trying to do this for the first time. In the process they will learn many things about themselves, their organisation and skills; they will gain confidence and experience, even if government policy does not change as a result of their actions. They will certainly be stronger and better prepared for future action and a resource to their community. If the funding organisation had simply worked through its representatives to exert influence through high-level political channels, the community group would have been deprived of the experience and lost the opportunity to extend their skills and experience. In fact, power would have been taken from the community.

Disabled people are not a homogeneous group, and an impairment of sight, hearing, learning ability, or physical mobility has specific implications for the affected individual. It is all too simple to involve a token disabled person for the sake of ideological respectability when, in fact, disabled people are a diverse group with a wide range of experiences, skills, and perceptions of their own identity. While a wheelchair-user may understand very well how to design a project that is accessible for wheelchairs, he or she may not know anything about the project-design implications for visually impaired people. An example of such a narrow perspective is the president of a Tuzla-based organisation of disabled people, who complained that a recent conference he had attended in Sarajevo was dominated by delegates from the capital itself. He was particularly concerned that there could never be a democratic system if regional and rural groups were not represented. Only when prompted on the issue of democratic structures and participation did he admit that only one woman had been present at the conference, and, in fact, her role was restricted to serving the refreshments.

Disability movements are often criticised for being fragmented and riddled with destructive internal politics. However, any movement — whether concerned with women's rights, civil rights, or environmental issues — also suffers from internal tensions. Perhaps this is a feature of human behaviour in groups and a reflection that most groups are not homogeneous, rather than a characteristic which should be particularly attributed to one movement. The stereotypes of disabled people commonly encountered in our society — the heroine struggling against the odds, the angel of purity and innocence, or the evil outsider, twisted and demented by his deformity — prevent us seeing the real person and both the positive and negative attributes of that person. After a UN agency meeting in Tuzla, the Chair praised the 'incredible and wonderful woman in the wheelchair' (although she couldn't remember her name), when in fact the woman in question had made a solid but unexceptional contribution to the meeting which should not have merited her being selected for praise or criticism any more than any other participant.

Discrimination and prejudice are as common among disabled people as in any other cross-section of society: racism, sexism, and homophobia are all present, and so is disablism. People with the most severe impairments, especially learning disabilities and impairments which affect conventional methods of communication, are particularly marginalised within the disability community. Any person who purports to represent a group of disabled people should have been elected by that group to represent their interests. Just as no individual woman can be seen as representing the views and needs of all women, it is a common mistake to assume that a single disabled person will represent all disabled people. Moreover, representatives of associations of disabled people do not necessarily represent the particular needs of disabled women; nor do women's groups necessarily represent the needs of minority groups of women such as the disabled, the elderly, and Romany women.

Change from within

In retrospect, it might be argued that the establishment of what was perceived as a separate 'disability unit' hampered the progress of Oxfam's Tuzla team as a whole towards a commitment to fair practices. The unit operated separately from the beginning, which made it difficult later to integrate disability into all areas of work. In relief distributions and work with women, attempts to see disability and prejudice as central issues have had limited success. Usha Kar, Country Representative for Bosnia from October 1994 to October 1996, describes the problems of working on prejudice at many levels and how this affected the formation of an integrated programme in Tuzla:

⁴ There is no objective 'measure' of prejudice — even identifying it is a subjective assessment. The difficulties encountered in overlaying work with women with disability issues, and vice versa, lay largely in a basic inability to understand that people have multiple identities and may be oppressed and disadvantaged on multiple levels. It was not until a focused effort was made to find disabled women and challenge the hierarchies of associations of disabled people that gender became an issue in disability work. The understanding of multiple levels of oppression did progress, and was reflected in the strategic planning process, during which in 1995 'women' and 'disabled people' were identified as vulnerable. By 1996 this had developed into a more sophisticated analysis of 'people with a lack of social networks', cross-cutting previously defined groups. ⁷

The management approach can be crucial in developing work on disability. Managers usually have the best access to resources, training, and additional support outside the field office, and are therefore in a prime position to develop new approaches within a staff team. It is also a managerial responsibility to ensure that needs-assessments are carried out, to analyse the external environment, and develop a strategic plan — all of which should take disability into account and form the basis for future actions and interventions.

Oxfam's *ad hoc* approach to disability and the system of line management means that one individual in a key position can present a block to effective work on disability issues. When this happened in the early days of the Tuzla programme, project staff felt very marginalised within the organisation, and some staff responsible for representing Oxfam's programme in the region actually knew very little about the work with disabled people. In advocacy, representation, networking, and fund-raising at a regional level, disability lacked the status of, for example, work with displaced women or ethnic minorities.

The line-management system within Oxfam consists of a series of managers supporting each other in a top-down chain. The system has many benefits; it has, for example, been very useful in allowing inexperienced staff members to gain management experience and skills. Its principal weakness is that one broken link in the chain can make the whole system dysfunctional. Within a line-management system, great care should be taken to ensure that staff members do not cut across the management structure and become directly involved in a project which is the responsibility of another manager. In Tuzla this rule was observed particularly strongly, because many Bosnian staff were first-time managers, and because there is a general tendency within Bosnian NGOs to make a direct approach to foreign staff, however inappropriate such an approach might be. Oxfam's line-management policy undoubtedly supported Bosnian staff in developing managerial skills; but it also created problems, because expatriate staff in key management positions, trying not to by-pass those with direct management responsibility, were often wrongly perceived as being uninterested in a particular project. However, it was the higher management which made final decisions on resource allocation and funding, and in Bosnia initially all higher management staff were expatriates. The lack of contact between project staff and higher-level management within Oxfam sometimes became a block to mutual understanding, as recalled by Cimeta Hatibovic, who helped to set up the Koraci Nade Centre:

> ❧ In the early days I thought the project wasn't very important to Oxfam and I was disappointed and demoralised by this. I had to beg for toys and all the other things we needed — a piece of carpet, for example. My advice to others is that, when you open a centre like this, there must be good co-operation and sharing of information between the office staff and the project staff. I needed to know about Oxfam and how it works too. ❧

Other members of the Tuzla team were not particularly aware of disability issues at the outset. This was partly due to lack of exposure, but sometimes due also to a significant lack of commitment to be even open-minded about disability — to the extent that some office staff expressed concerns about working with a disabled colleague. When the management staff introduced firm guidelines on disablism, individuals were less likely to express their thoughts in front of other staff who did not share their opinion. It was generally understood that it was unacceptable for Oxfam staff members to make racist, disablist, or sexist comments; but such comments were seen as harmless fun, rather than a contradiction of the principles and policies of the organisation. When a disability-equity trainer came to carry out a consultancy in Tuzla, a session was arranged for the staff team; but the team felt pre-judged by the trainer, and the trainer was disappointed by the lack of open-mindedness, and so no progress was made. A consistent management approach that promotes disability awareness on a daily basis is much more effective than brief training 'spurts' where the trainer lacks sufficient time to build a relationship of openness with trainees. The process of raising awareness within Oxfam Tuzla has been a continual effort over the past two years, and still has some way to go yet.

Equality of opportunity

The introduction of equal opportunities in recruitment had begun in 1994. The concept of equal opportunities was new to Bosnia and to most of the original staff, who had not themselves been through a rigidly fair recruitment process. This was probably one of the most controversial issues for the Tuzla team to deal with, especially in relation to disability. In Bosnia there had been no such culture before the war, and in the war the practice of exploiting personal connections and favours, especially for family members, was very strong. The effects of the war meant that everyone was desperate for any kind of income, and having a friend or relative working for an aid agency was often seen as the entry point for most of the family, who put intense pressure on the working member. The commitment that an aid agency can expect of its staff is far weaker than the pressures of family loyalty, especially in extreme situations such as war-time.

The difficulty of working on the principle of equal opportunities is that it relies on cultural norms from Western Europe which might not be appropriate, or may even be against the law in some countries. The problems in Bosnia began first with the process of drawing up recruitment criteria and extended to the use of application forms and references, and to the interview itself. Previous normal practice did not fit in with methods designed to ensure equal opportunities: national staff had felt it was acceptable for all to read and discuss applications and make enquiries about the family and character of the applicant. Most applicants outlined their personal connections on the application form. Although contacts in local government, the police and the military were actually very useful, they could not fairly be considered as recruitment criteria. However, staff members who did coincidentally have connections in useful places sometimes found it a lot easier to carry out their jobs — in getting official permission to drive to another town, and certainly in avoiding mobilisation into the army!

The job application form had to be re-designed several times to ensure that the instructions were clear. Often only those who had worked for other international agencies were able to fill it in. The most difficult part was an open section at the end, asking applicants to outline their interests, skills, and experience in relation to the selection criteria; this was often left blank or contained irrelevant information. Applicants frequently undersold themselves on paper, yet the application form was used to select candidates for interview. This still poses a barrier to many people and provokes debate within the office. For example, a logistician will have to be able to use standard forms which she or he may never have used before as part of their job: a properly completed application form indicates an ability to fill in paperwork. If an applicant omits to complete a crucial part of a job application, this might indicate a lack of attention to important detail which is an essential part of the job. In a situation where large numbers of people apply for each post, there has to be a basis on which to select the few who will be interviewed. Within equal-opportunities systems there is flexibility for each country office to adopt more culturally appropriate methods of recruitment which do not discriminate against those who have no experience of Western European systems, but are well able to carry out the job. The Bosnia teams are still working towards overcoming the barrier of the application form.

In Tuzla the whole team participated creatively in finding different locations to advertise new jobs where disabled people, displaced people, women, and older people gathered. One time the advertisement even stated that Oxfam encouraged suitably qualified people from these groups to apply; but the feedback showed that most people were puzzled by this statement, and the profile of applicants for that particular post was not significantly different from other sets of applicants.

Attitudinal barriers

As it became increasingly clear that attitudinal barriers and ethnic nationalism within the team were adversely affecting the programme, attitudes towards partner groups such as disabled people, Roma people, minority groups, and rural displaced people became the main essential criteria for recruitment.

Usha Kar explains the problems of trying to introduce equal opportunities practice in Tuzla:

❛ The core of equal opportunities lies with attitude: it's not just about implementing a set of procedures, although they act as some kind of check or balance. It needs a real commitment to trying to ensure that people gain fair access to their entitlements. In this sense people, including staff members, can only be 'trained' to a certain extent. In Bosnia, in a war context where jobs and goods were exceptionally prized, and where traditionally social advantages were gained through connections and subjective factors, the application of objective criteria in recruitment and service delivery was (a) viewed with suspicion and disbelief, (b) an unfamiliar concept, and (c) contrary to the formerly established system. At the same time, it was even more important to apply equal opportunities to ensure that Oxfam was not considered partisan. For example, when employing people it was important to be sure that decisions were based on skills, not ethnic group, age, sex, etc. The process of implementing the equal-opportunities policy was slow, because the starting point was one of unfamiliarity with the concept and a poor understanding of its importance. ❜

However, the pressure to find new staff who are skilled in a particular job still means that sometimes people whose personal opinions are not acceptable are recruited into the organisation. An example frequently encountered in field offices is the male logistician who firmly believes that women cannot drive and makes his opinions clear to his female colleagues, yet is a very experienced logistician who in many other ways would be a great asset to the organisation. It is unrealistic to pretend that 'awareness training' can be provided later on the job, or that deep-rooted prejudices will disappear overnight. Feedback from recently recruited Oxfam field staff shows that the new recruitment and interview practices made them feel very clear about what Oxfam was expecting in terms of their personal attitude, especially with regard to disability.

'Desirable' criteria such as knowledge of English, and ability to drive or use a computer *can* be taught on the job if necessary. There are many groups of people in society whose access to education or the employment market has been limited for various reasons, but introducing posts for trainees can help applicants who lack the relevant experience and skills to join the organisation. For a field office on a very tight budget, the lower salary for a trainee allows the difference between that and the full-post salary to be used for training. While more established offices may have other sources of funds for staff development, the experience in Tuzla has shown that an organisation can have a strong commitment to staff training on paper; but limited training budgets do not necessarily allow that commitment to be put into practice. Positive action which brings about a noticeable change within an organisation shows that a commitment to working on disability issues has begun already, and is the first step to building a partnership with individuals and groups of disabled people.

When the two children's centres in Tuzla were joined together to become Koraci Nade, all posts in the new Centre were reviewed and re-advertised. Some staff re-applied for jobs in the new Centre, but others did not want to work on a project where the focus was on integration. The primary purpose of re-advertising all posts was to ensure that in the recruitment process the attitudes of the staff were positive about the goals of the project. In order to achieve its aims, the Centre needed a whole team committed to the rights of the child and to the process of integration. Realistically it would have been difficult to find any staff able to work with a group of severely disabled children who did not approach disability from a medical angle: after all, it was the only approach before the war, and no examples of other options were available. The compromise was to recruit staff who were *open to learning* about new approaches and willing to try a different way of working. From the testimonies of staff members such as Fata, Jasmina, and Azra in the previous chapters, it is obvious that this was very difficult, especially in the beginning, when they felt confused and disempowered in their work. However, they did persevere, and they did give a chance to a very new approach and now can see positive results from their experiences. In fact, Fata declared that she would never work in the old way again, so pleased was she with the results of an integrated environment:

> ❧ I had quite a bad experience when I started working in the Oxfam Centre. I was used to a system where we had a separate specialist for each different condition, and I found it really difficult to work with a group of children of mixed disabilities and age-groups. Now, though, I can really see how all the children learn better from each other and how much progress they are making. I am really happy in my job, especially when I see the results of working like this. ❧

The introduction of a different way of working is difficult in any situation: new ideas, while adopted by some, are greeted with hostility by others who feel threatened by them. A key element when promoting a social model of disability is, as this chapter has argued, to put your own house in order first.

Basically any agency should be looking at its internal policies and ways of working on a day-to-day basis. What factors about the organisation prevent disabled people from being full and equal partners?

Physical barriers

For Oxfam Tuzla there were many such issues. The team was dominated by urban, educated, non-disabled young people, initially recruited as much for their knowledge of the English language as anything else. The office was inaccessible to wheelchair-users: it had steps to the entrance and the toilets were small and squat. Some of the systems used in the office would have made it exceptionally difficult for a blind or deaf staff member to participate equally in the team. After a year of negotiations, a ramp was finally built at the rear door, as a busy main road in front of the building made it impossible to build a ramp in front. On principle the Oxfam office wanted the ramp to be part of the front entrance, but the landlords would under no circumstances allow it, and in any case it would have been impossible without expensive structural changes. As negotiations continued over the months, Oxfam's disabled partners said that a rear entrance was better than no entrance at all, and a compromise was reached. The rear door, however, was often locked by the managers of the premises. Some of Oxfam's offices in Former Yugoslavia are still not accessible to wheelchair-users, and there are some Oxfam staff members who are reluctant to spend any part of a tight budget on accessibility. This not only prevents disabled staff and partners from actually entering the office; it also undermines Oxfam's attempts to influence change and campaign for accessibility in public buildings. It has also brought about charges of hypocrisy from Oxfam partners, and is a prime example of the unwillingness of some individuals to take disability seriously, and the organisation's lack of clear policy on obliging all offices to meet minimum standards.

Once the Tuzla office moved towards increasingly targeting disabled people in recruitment, several new disabled staff members in both the office and project teams were recruited. Each office had to think about ways of changing the furniture around to make room for wheelchairs, about the best height for the photocopier, and how the Braille reports produced by a visually impaired staff member would be translated and written down in the local language. Each disabled staff member was paid a disability allowance, based on estimates of the cost of additional support needed to enable that person to travel to work. The employment contract used in the Former Yugoslavia was reviewed and rewritten to emphasise clearly what support would be given to disabled staff. However, once practical problems were largely dealt with, attitudinal barriers continued to be a problem for disabled staff members.

Kaca Sarihodzic began working for Oxfam in January 1996, when attempts to deal with disablism in the field office were at their peak.

> ❝ I was really pleased to have an opportunity to work for Oxfam. I didn't think I would ever get a job again after my accident. I used to work in the Municipality offices, but they weren't interested in having me back once I became a wheelchair-user. At first Oxfam gave me really good support — getting transport, giving me extra financial support for personal assistance. But once I started working in Oxfam, I began to have problems about transport, because some of the staff weren't so willing to help me after a while. They made it clear that I was a problem for them. ❞

A clear policy and training for all staff should stress that disabled members of staff have a basic right to a certain level of assistance to enable them to carry out their jobs. When other staff members are responsible for giving this assistance, there is a real risk of power-play — especially when individual conflicts and personality clashes occur. There should be a clear demarcation between the individual interaction between two colleagues and the basic rights of a disabled staff member.

Policy and planning for an alternative approach

Lack of awareness about disability was a block to work with disabled people in Tuzla, but what is really lacking in Oxfam across the whole organisation is a disability policy. The adoption of a policy would ensure that all staff members were aware of their rights and how they were expected to behave in daily interactions. It would also provide essential management tools for analysis and planning and put a clear obligation on a team manager, rather than leaving the initiative to individual preference or interest.

A UNHCR workshop on assistance to disabled refugees (in Pakistan, 1992) discussed what kinds of response would be appropriate to meet the needs of disabled people in emergency situations. One of the central recommendations from this workshop was the need for staff training, both in practical assistance and in the organisation's policies and guidelines. The workshop recognised that, without awareness of the needs of a marginalised group, no agency can expect the staff members who are implementing a response or project to be able to meet those needs. Furthermore the particular approach of staff will crucially affect the method of implementation: there are many different ways to carry out a relief distribution, for example. The attitudes and beliefs of staff members and their compatibility with the organisation's working principles can make the difference between a successful project, carried out in line with the organisational policy, and an unsuccessful project, or even a disastrous one. By ensuring that it has clear policies an organisation can make sure that its approach is consistent — that what its head office states in advocacy and public relations work matches what actually happens in the field.

Oxfam Tuzla was working with disabled people long before the changes in the internal structures were made, although ideally it should have been the other way round. The visit of the Disability Adviser in March 1994 was the beginning of Tuzla's work with disabled people, and of the development of a plan or strategy for working with disabled people. Strategic planning enabled the team as a whole to become involved in developing a deeper understanding of disability. It also gave field staff clear direction and guidelines for project design and implementation. Key questions could be considered, such as: should we work with institutions even if they adopt an exclusively medical approach? Should we work with groups of military disabled people? How can we meet urgent relief needs *and* promote longer-term change? With limited resources and capacity, where should we start in order to be most effective?

In Bosnia Oxfam was an organisation with a clear approach to disability, trying to work in an environment where a totally different approach — an institutional approach — was prevalent. This extract from a report by Helen Lee following a visit to neighbouring Serbia in July 1994 looks at the problem:

❦ How does Oxfam contribute to an improved quality of life for disabled people living in institutions? This is the challenge. I feel that we cannot ignore the existence of such places, yet need to be realistic about what we can actually achieve that goes beyond short-term help in the form of humanitarian aid.

Institutions are well-known for the deeply entrenched attitudes held by the majority of staff which make any change threatening and difficult. The staff can be as institutionalised as the people who live there and closed to new ideas and ways of looking at things. Without a willingness to change on their part, any chance of improving people's lives is impossible. Somehow we need to involve the staff in a process that is liberating for them as well as for disabled people. Very often staff have internalised the negative attitudes of society towards disabled people and see no value in what they do. I feel that we need first to identify institutions where there are signs of willingness to change and develop; and particularly at the top, because without the manager's co-operation there is no chance of success. We then need to look at concrete ways of contributing to a better quality of life for residents. This could be through training for staff which encourages them to relate more positively and creatively to the people in their care. **7**

From recommendations made by advisers, discussions with disabled people, and meetings with heads of institutions and other agencies, an overview of the situation was drawn up and areas identified where Oxfam Tuzla could be most effective. There were a number of associations of disabled people, but they had been closely linked to the State in the past, and were focused primarily on getting aid to their members. There were few suitable local partners, and Oxfam carried out all work as operational projects, with the aim of promoting the development of local NGOs. A Disability Strategy was drafted in October 1994 which covered five key areas where Oxfam felt it could have an impact:

- The support and strengthening of local organisations of disabled people — through organisational development, the provision of material needs and enabling aids, and support of income-generating activities.
- The provision of services, such as the Children's Support Centre and the outreach component.
- The integration of disability into Oxfam's general programme — drafting a disability policy for the office, awareness-training for staff in gender and disability issues, and appropriate relief distributions for disabled people.
- Disability awareness in the community — training for trainers in associations of disabled people, advocacy, and dissemination (including translation) of information.
- Support to appropriate institutions for disabled people where there is a willingness for change.

Since then Oxfam Tuzla has funded NGO development training, has distributed wheelchairs and other aids, and has continued to fund the Koraci Nade Centre. While Oxfam in Tuzla has not given financial support to businesses run by associations of disabled people — other agencies have taken on that role — some books and magazines have been translated and distributed, although more are needed on a regular basis; and considerable advocacy work has been carried out at the field level. The original assessment has therefore given not only direction to the disability work, but also some indicators to use for checking progress and carrying out reviews and evaluations in future. The planning process has also ensured that Oxfam's work does not duplicate the work of other agencies, nor does it miss out large areas of need. In 1996 the strategic planning session with staff, partners, and individual disabled people produced a chart (Figure 1, oppposite) exploring the causes of poverty and powerlessness among disabled people, and ways to address the root causes. The chart is not definitive, but it represents a starting point, and is specific to the situation in Bosnia (although many parts of it are more broadly applicable). What it does show is a progression from a position where disability was not really considered as an issue for many of the people who participated, to attempts to make a detailed analysis in a relatively short period of time. From a situation in 1994 in which just two or three staff members within the 'disability unit' defined policy and planned implementation, two years later all the staff team, project partners, and individual disabled people participated in the process of analysis and planning.

By the time that the 1996–2001 Strategic Plan was drafted in conjunction with partners, project staff, and office staff, 21 specific interventions were identified to '*reduce vulnerability and isolation by creating the conditions and environment whereby identified poor, marginalised, disadvantaged, and isolated people can proactively work towards gaining more choice and control in their lives*'. These identified interventions included regular updating and revision of internal practice and policy, as well as specific projects and advocacy work, and they incorporated work with people who were socially marginalised by age, disability, ethnicity or any other discriminating factor. As the situation in Bosnia changed and improved for some people, there was an increasing need to prioritise within target groups and recognise that not all disabled, elderly, or displaced people were in the same situation. The lack of a social network and the absence of family and community support were defined as some of the most important factors in the creation of poverty and powerlessness.

Conclusion

It is clear that dealing with disability involves first examining internal structures — especially attitudinal barriers and discrimination. Any organisation that takes disability seriously needs to ensure that its recruitment procedure examines the attitudes of applicants. Some attitudinal barriers are simply the result of lack of knowledge. As in the example of the Koraci Nade staff, identifying people who are open to learn and open to change is one solution if discriminatory attitudes are widespread in society. However, we should be wary of recruiting staff with a negative attitude to disabled people, women, ethnic minorities, or other groups with the idea of carrying out awareness-training later. This rarely happens in fact, and is often used as a way

Figure 1

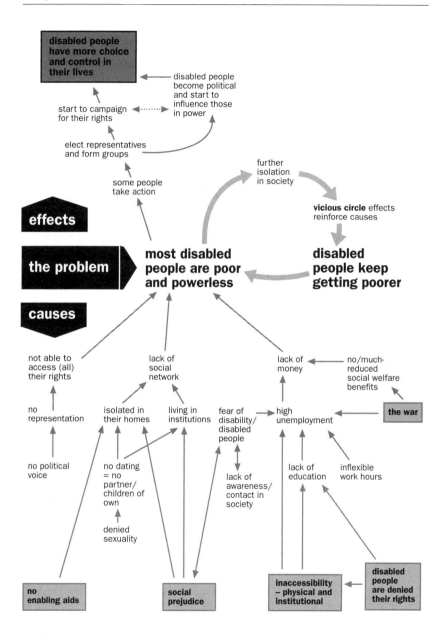

to avoid facing up to the real issue. If challenging attitudinal barriers in society is actually part of the organisation's programme, then effective action and change will be achieved only if all staff are fully committed to the purpose. Not only does the recruitment procedure need to take attitude into account, but every organisation needs to have a clear policy on discrimination and a way of enforcing this policy: all staff need to be clear and understand what is expected from them and why. Creative thinking and advice from disabled people can help to tackle architectural and institutional barriers which prevent disabled people from participating — although we all need to be aware of the dangers of tokenism, and aim for full and equal participation. In the experience of the Tuzla team, having the support of a disability adviser was invaluable in defining policy and planning, and providing a source of advice and a channel to reach other organisations. Field managers are another essential part of the process in influencing daily work and interactions. The process of moving disability from the margins to the centre of Oxfam's work is slow and laborious, primarily due to the lack of organisational commitment which has left field staff unsupported on disability issues; but there are areas where analysis, policy change, and planning are happening, and this should help to keep disability firmly on Oxfam's agenda.

Promoting an alternative approach to disability in Bosnia 5

Oxfam's approach to disability has provoked a mixed reaction among partners and professionals in Bosnia. All over Eastern Europe attitudes towards disability have been centred on the medical solution to the 'problem' of disabled people. In the communist system in Yugoslavia, which allowed much more individual freedom than those countries more closely aligned with the Soviet Union, institutions were considered the 'solution'. Throughout Yugoslavia there were a number of large institutions and special schools, where children and adults from all regions received medical and developmental care. The term 'defectologist', denoting a professional working with disabled people, gives a clear indication of the approach common in Bosnia. Disabled people were predominantly seen as the responsibility of the health-services system and were 'categorised' by medical professionals. This categorisation defined all the social welfare support that an individual could receive. The pre-war health-care system operated through a network of clinics, hospitals, public-health centres, and institutions. Even before the war there were problems in the existing health system, as outlined in a WHO/Ministry of Health report: '*The pre-war health system suffered from a number of problems. A supply-dominated approach to centralised planning led to the proliferation of large hospitals and heavy reliance on specialised poly-clinics, with relatively little attention to primary health care or family practice. The centralised decision-making process did little to encourage strategic planning to achieve the most efficient use of resources. Instead, decisions were often the result of bureaucratic bargaining rather than a rational assessment of needs and available resources. Clinical decisions were not based on considerations of the effectiveness or costs of the desired interventions.*'

Many of the institutions and clinics are in Serbia and Croatia and, since the break-up of Former Yugoslavia, they have no automatic obligations to Bosnian citizens. In fact, there are reports that some disabled children have recently returned to Tuzla from institutions in Serbia which are not willing to continue to meet the cost of caring for Bosnian children when resources are already stretched in meeting the needs of Serbian children.

What do disabled people want?

One of the main problems created by concentrating control of services for disabled people in the hands of medical professionals is the overwhelming disparity between what medical professionals think disabled people need and what disabled people themselves want. Oxfam's disabled partners in Bosnia frequently express their sense of frustration when confronted with the fact that service-provision for disabled people is largely controlled by non-disabled people. A professional defectologist probably spoke for most State-employed specialists when describing a vision of clean, large, and well-equipped institutions: special schools and clinics with all the latest equipment *'as you have in Britain'*. This same professional is very sceptical about the possibility of integrated schooling, while conceding that special units within regular schools might just be workable in selected areas.

In Bosnia there are mixed opinions about institutions. The experiences and opinions of less disabled people tend to differ from those of severely disabled people. People who spent their childhood in institutional care and are now living at home are usually those who have milder impairments or are able to communicate and move around relatively easily. They speak of institutions without much criticism, often with great respect, sometimes even with fondness. Most children found it difficult to live away from their families, but had no friends near their homes and longed to get back to the institution at the end of school holidays. Only now are they and their families beginning to question the necessity of an institution-based system.

Predictably, those people who have the most severe impairments, have very limited mobility, and do not communicate in the usual way are at greater risk of abuse and mistreatment in institutions. At the very least, the failure of staff to understand their needs causes immense frustration; but maltreatment and abuse by staff who do not attempt to communicate with severely disabled individuals is all too common.

Edina Barjaktarevic, a young woman who has used a wheelchair since a car accident 19 years ago, has a very different vision of the future. She described the institution where she spent much of her childhood from the age of nine years: *'It felt as though I was in jail; it didn't feel like home at all'*. She sees a future where, from birth, disabled and non-disabled children play together, learn together and from each other, supported by services available within the community. She would like a future where all children learn sign and Braille in school, where television programmes are subtitled and have sign-language inserts. Edina did not encounter any particular problems in the institution, and spoke about it quite fondly — but in retrospect she cannot understand why she was sent 150 km from her home and family to be educated in an institution along with over 100 other children:

> ❛ They [the local council] have paid out so much money for all these years to keep me in an institution — wouldn't it have been cheaper and better for everyone if they had built a few ramps in the school and offered me accessible transport? ❜

Integration has proved to be one of the most debated aspects of Oxfam's attempts to promote the social-model approach to disability. However, there is a growing awareness that, as Bosnia is rebuilt after the war, it does not have to revert to the old system — and that community groups can try to influence government policy. War-disabled people are becoming particularly prominent in the gradually emerging disability 'movement'. The social model assumes a role for community groups and service-users in defining service-provision, but in the pre-war communist system this was not an option. Not only were there no independent systems to represent the needs of the community: many people felt then and still feel today that they cannot influence government policy. Groups such as the Association of Mothers of Handicapped Children are beginning to see an advocacy role for themselves, but many disabled people and parents of disabled children do not feel that it is their responsibility, or that they have the power to change anything. The idea of a non-government sector in Bosnia is very new, and only after two years are local NGOs seeing a long-term role for themselves in advocacy work and the promotion of human rights, rather than simply meeting the material/relief needs of their members. The change to a community-based approach may be introduced from above by the Ministry of Health in co-ordination with advisers such as the World Health Organisation, but it cannot succeed unless individuals and groups feel some responsibility to the community and have adequate independent systems to monitor and influence government from below.

What do carers really want?

Sajda Arnautovic is a member of a World Health Organisation working group on disability and the main driving force behind the Association of Mothers of Handicapped Children. Her son, Damir, attends the Koraci Nade Centre. The Association of Mothers was started partly in response to the Koraci Nade Centre's inability to provide sufficient support to parents of disabled children — a need which several staff there acknowledged — and bad experiences of institutional care. Sajda believes not only that institutions are inappropriate, but that they are the perfect environment for abuse, and told me about her son's experience of two institutions several hours' drive from Tuzla.

> ❢ I will give you an example from Damir's life. When he was about five years old he was just trying to learn to walk. It was the normal thing for severely disabled children to be sent to institutions, and I had no one to look after him at home. Anyway I went to see him after he had been there 15 days and took him some chocolate, which he loves. When I arrived, he was strapped to some kind of strange chair that I can't explain; his head was in an abnormal position and he had a rash all over his neck. I tried to give him the chocolate, but he wasn't interested, he couldn't communicate with me any more, and I knew something was wrong, that he was frightened and he was being treated badly. I couldn't complain to anyone, and finally after two months I just took him in my arms and carried him out of there. He was also in another institution near Sarajevo. I always used to call before I went to visit him, but one time I couldn't get through so I just turned up. I found him in a terrible condition; he was covered in urine, even his shoes were full of urine, he had excrement smeared in his hair and his ear and he was blue with cold — I had to take him straight to hospital. ❞

Now the Association of Mothers promotes care and service-provision in the community, so that severely disabled children can live at home with their families. Sajda feels that mothers know their children better than any professional — that a mother can always tell when her child is hungry, thirsty, or needs to go to the toilet. The training of defectologists as yet does not seem to include an understanding of how severely disabled people can communicate through a special form of sign language. Lack of knowledge about how people can communicate their needs other than by verbal language means that many severely disabled people are left to defecate in their beds. There are signs that such a system will be introduced to Bosnia in the future. Meanwhile, Sajda's response is to promote the role of parents, especially the mother, in caring for a disabled child. She would like to see more mothers employed in centres like Koraci Nade and their skills and experience being respected as much as those of professional defectologists. The Association of Women and the Association of Mothers (which grew out of the Association of Women) are the only organisations which are specifically concerned with women and disability, though from the point of view of women as carers, rather than focusing on the experiences, needs, and rights of disabled women and girls.

While the Association of Mothers promotes the role of the home environment and family, Sajda also acknowledges a central criticism of community-based rehabilitation: that the family environment is not automatically the healthiest place for a child to grow and develop. Just as abuse and mistreatment can happen in institutions, social stigma can also lead to mistreatment in the home. Sajda would like to see a whole range of options for care in the community, and disabled children living at home to be seen as active members of their community:

> ❧ Each child is individual, and institution staff don't know the needs of each child. What I would like to see promoted in services for disabled children is a more homely atmosphere, a place where everyone can have fun as well. I would also like to see an end to the idea that a family should be ashamed of a disabled child. The consequences of this can be terrible. I came across a woman of 37 years who had never been seen by anyone but her immediate family. She only weighed 30 kg, and her family wouldn't even let me see her at first. I had to go to the house after dark. ❧

Sajda sees a strong role for mothers of severely disabled children in campaigning for changes in Bosnia. But just as much as parents like Sajda want to see fewer professionals working in the Centre, representatives of regional services for disabled people criticise Koraci Nade for not having *enough* professionals working there. It is a hard balance to achieve, and in the end it may be that no one is completely satisfied.

New roles for rehabilitation professionals

There are signs that attitudes are beginning to change among professionals. Rehabilitation specialists have started to conceive their role in broader terms, especially their role in influencing government policy. I spoke to the Director of the Kosta Popov School for Children with Learning Difficulties, Muharem Osmic. Oxfam has distributed clothing and shoes to children in the school during the war, but the directorate feel that Oxfam should have done more for the school, and they are very wary of Oxfam's approach. However, he told me:

> ❧ In the future I think special schools like this one will be safe, but I would like to see certain children integrated into regular schools. Special schools should just be for children with the most severe impairments. But the government needs to provide funds for the costs of integration, and it will be a process of 10 to 15 years. Before the war, the reform process in education had begun, our schools were moving more towards

the models that we see in Western Europe, but now the war and reconstruction have set us back and held up the reform process. **❜**

Despite this, others nearer to the grassroots feel that the post-war reconstruction process is the ideal opportunity to introduce reform. Jasmina Suljagic is a student of defectology and employed as a trainee physiotherapist at the Centre.

❛ Before the war we didn't have anything like this; there were just institutions and special schools. In centres like this the children are close to their families and it's fun, because they learn and develop through games. Many other kids are closed in by four walls. Here they can develop with other children. Look at Martina [a young girl who attends the Centre] for example: before she came here, she had spent most of her life just with her grandparents and she was afraid of other children. Now she loves it here and can play with other children. This Centre has a role in educating society. **❜**

Views among other professionals are also changing. Students from the Faculty of Defectology say that the Centre is the place where they have learnt most about how to work with disabled children. They will be the professionals of the future and are seeing a whole new approach in practice. Medina Vantic, a third-year student, chose to study defectology after working as a physio-therapist in a local medical rehabilitation unit.

❛ I have been coming to the Centre for a year now, and what I like is that the theory and practice come together. The only real practice I get is here in the Centre. The other options are just medical units or hospitals. Segregation is not good, but it's society that has the problems. I'm just not sure how open normal children are to accepting it. **❜**

Unfortunately very few people who are themselves disabled or have disabled family members become defectologists. One disabled women told me she would like to study defectology, but access presents a problem for her — although the Faculty would be supportive to disabled students. One exception is Azra Begtasagovic, a physiotherapist in the Koraci Nade Centre, who is visually impaired. Her attitude towards disability and her hopes for the future are a result of her own experiences as a child and her work in the Koraci Nade Centre.

❛ At nine years old I had a brain tumour removed and after that I had problems with my eyes. Before the operation I was one of the clever kids in a normal school, and it was thanks to my teacher that I could return to my school afterwards. I was in a normal school and my friends accepted my impairment. As I moved up into the higher classes, my first teacher just told the new teacher what kind of help I needed and how I could work. I finished junior school with no problems, but then at secondary school there was one teacher who wouldn't help me: the mathematics teacher wouldn't let my friend at the next desk read what was on the blackboard for me. He threw me out of his class and told me to go to the hospital, where I belonged. I couldn't stay at the school after that and I was sent to a special school in Belgrade. It was strange for me, having come from a normal school, but I was flexible and soon adapted. In fact I had quite a nice time there, although it was hard to be away from my parents. My opinion is that I was just like any other child — it was the maths teacher who needed educating. Teachers need to learn how to be flexible in their methods, or they will be the ones handicapped by their attitudes.

When I came to work at the Oxfam Centre, I remember that lots of people were sceptical about Oxfam's approach, but now they have started to change their opinions. When I told other professionals what we were doing and how we were working, they were surprised. Now they even refer children here from the Health Centre, and students from the Faculty are coming for teaching practice. The scepticism from other professionals was because they feel threatened by something new; plus we got paid more money than them.

We lived under a very different system and learned to work in a very different way. In the beginning it was very hard: we learned only to work with just one child, do our thing and then say goodbye. I see it like this: when you are trained all your life to put a certain object in one place, it becomes like a reflex, and when you try to change and put it somewhere else, it's very hard and disturbing. Luckily most of the staff here were willing to be open and we can see the results of that. Now I couldn't work in any other way. I only know one thing: before the war, children in Bosnia needed a centre like this. It's sad that it took a war for us to get this. I'd like to see lots more centres working on this approach and I would encourage anyone to be open-minded and try it. Working here has changed my view of what it means to be a professional. No one else accepts these children, no one wants them. Here they learn through games and play, they enjoy the Centre. I hope to see more of this approach in the future. I hope that it will change our consciousness, that it will change Bosnia. ❜

85

The local authorities

One of the problems now faced by Oxfam Tuzla in trying to achieve long-term sustainability for its disability projects is its poor relationship with local authorities and rehabilitation professionals. While attempts have been made to increase co-operation, generally there is a feeling that Oxfam has always gone its own way and not wanted to support professionals in Bosnia. There is some truth in this: certainly Oxfam did not want to perpetuate the *status quo* and support institution which did not respect the rights of users. Many aspects of Oxfam's work have been very controversial and considered radical — especially the idea of integration. Its support of parents, volunteers, and community structures in their efforts to develop a stronger voice in demanding appropriate service-provision has been seen as threatening by some of those in positions of power. By making clear its opposition to an institutional approach, Oxfam has alienated itself from the heads of institutions, who felt personally attacked. But ironically they are actually beginning to change their attitudes. One member of a Tuzla-based organisation told me:

> ❜ They will never ever admit it, but Oxfam has had a lot of influence on their attitudes. Even if they don't completely believe it, they at least have the sense to see that it's the way forward — it's going to happen anyway and many other agencies will support them if they make moves in the right direction. But they won't go back to Oxfam and say, 'Sorry, I was wrong. Can we work together now?' ❜

Echoing this comment, other agencies have also acknowledged that the work which Oxfam has done in the past now makes it possible for them, two years later, to implement their own projects.

Oxfam had already identified a need for change in institutions, but a lack of capacity and resources and an uncertainty about how to move forward in the face of hostility meant that little was done in this area. Additionally the International Rescue Committee from the USA had a programme of support to institutions with their own physiotherapist, Mary Lou Hunt. Rather than duplicate IRC's work, the two organisations worked in close co-operation:

> ❜ The work of Oxfam and IRC really complement each other — we are just working in different physical environments to the same end. The link into the community is very important and the working relationship is very good, because we are all therapists. IRC is working within the system to change it, and Oxfam is introducing something new to the system through the community. ❜

However, Mary Lou and her colleague, Laura Hamilton, an occupational therapist, have found resistance to new ideas a problem on occasion:

❧ When we first came here, we had to do hands-on work for the first six months to prove ourselves. The philosophy of approach to, for example, a neurological trauma, would follow a strict sequence: first the patient would learn to crawl — not just to crawl, in fact, but to crawl perfectly before moving on to learning to walk again. There is a strong belief in a developmental sequence. There was a resistance to the ideas that we presented of how things could be done differently, and money was always used as an excuse, but in fact our methods were low-tech and low-cost. ❧

The Faculty of Defectology

Before the war, most professionals were trained in Belgrade in Serbia, although there had been plans to establish a Faculty of Defectology in Tuzla. When the war started, many professionals left Bosnia and returned to Serbia, prompting Tuzla to try to open its own Faculty in the midst of the war. In 1993, the Tuzla Faculty of Defectology opened, following the pre-war plan, but without the necessary resources. The Faculty faced huge problems, not just finding in a physical space, books and study materials, but also in finding teachers. Cimeta Hatibovic, who helped to set up the Koraci Nade Centre, was asked to become a part-time lecturer at the Faculty, surviving on her Oxfam salary, as the lecturing posts were all unpaid. When the Faculty first opened, many young men enrolled to study Defectology as a way to avoid being mobilised into the army. About 400 people signed up, but in fact so far there have only been 200 real students; those avoiding mobilisation were not really interested in the subject.

'Defectology' as a term has prompted much comment and is generally seen to embody the 'medical model' attitude towards disabled people in Bosnia. However, times are changing and so is language. Cimeta told me:

❧ We have contacts with lecturers in Zagreb and hope that they will come to lecture here in Tuzla. We also have very good links with the University of Bologna and we hope to make many more contacts all over the world now that the war is over. A big part of our future is integration and social rehabilitation — it is the only way forward. We would also like to change the name of the Faculty to reflect our new priorities and ways of working — something that relates to integration and social aspects of rehabilitation. This is a new faculty and has many more opportunities to be progressive and bring new ideas to Bosnia. ❧

Even though Oxfam has not had a good direct relationship with the Faculty of Defectology, the staff employed in the Koraci Nade Centre have always been very involved in the Faculty, and many are teachers there. In this way Oxfam has managed to exert an influence within the Faculty, and individuals who rejected the notion of integration two years ago are now actively promoting it. I spoke with a young American physiotherapist who is working on a WHO-supported Community-Based Rehabilitation project in northern Bosnia. Having worked with professional therapists all over Bosnia, he was amazed by the way the Koraci Nade Centre was working, calling it *'a real CBR programme from the grassroots'*. He was impressed too by the attitudes and ideas of the staff.

Although Oxfam's work is strongly supported by disabled people themselves, and the Koraci Nade Centre provides services that simply would not have been supplied otherwise, the lack of a constructive dialogue with representatives of the State system is likely to have negative effects for at least the Koraci Nade Centre. Somewhere along the line, even though Oxfam's approach is the opposite of the State approach, a dialogue should have been better established in which the two parties could agree to disagree, but remain in contact. Within each culture the way to do this will be different: direct methods may not always work and can create open hostility; more diplomatic methods may need to be used, in order to maintain respect on both parts.

Other agencies

During the war in Bosnia many of the roles of the State were taken on by aid agencies, and they constitute a complete distinct sector to take into consideration. Every agency exists within a 'development community' and relies on other agencies to a certain extent — much more so in emergency programmes, when they can give each other mutual support in terms of logistics and accommodation, and transport and security arrangements such as travelling in convoy with other agencies.

In terms of co-ordination and effectiveness, each individual project is located within the context of an overall approach. Each agency's approach is countered or complemented not only by the local or State structure, but also by the other agencies operational in that area. New agencies often have to prove their credibility by carrying out relief distributions and investing a certain sum of money to supply State-defined needs (where they correspond with the agency's own assessment). It is also an important factor in building a relationship with the community: while disabled people lack basic medical and nutritional supplies, physical comfort, suitable clothing, and hygiene items, they will not be in a position to play a role in a developmental project.

Just as without a wheelchair someone who is paraplegic cannot attend a meeting to lobby for his or her rights, another person concerned primarily with trying to get enough food for his or her family will not have the time or energy to devote to awareness campaigns.

A small-budget, low-profile agency may focus on persuading a more influential organisation to take on some of the issues it is working on, in order to gain additional support and profile. In Tuzla a Disability Working Group was set up by UNHCR for the co-ordination of work with disabled people, yet there was no representative of disabled people present. When Oxfam staff lobbied for a disabled person to be present, they were told that it would be acceptable as long as the person in question would be '*diplomatic*'. The same UNHCR representative required Oxfam to prove that ramps were '*economically viable*' before agreeing to consider supporting Oxfam's efforts to influence international agencies involved in reconstruction and construction projects. (Unfortunately the same reasoning is used by some Oxfam staff for not taking the trouble to ensure that their offices are accessible to disabled staff and partners.) Although UNHCR had well-known policies defining its support for disabled people, the attitude of an individual staff member was able to block action. This again illustrates the need for every organisation to have a policy and to be sure that their staff members uphold and represent that policy in word and action. It also shows how limited one agency can be when it relies on the support of others who do not share the same priorities.

The Italian Red Cross has co-operated closely with Oxfam in the development of it construction projects in Bosnia. The IRC has considered carefully the social and community implications of their projects involving special schools and institutions, and has succeeded in retaining a close and constructive relationship with local government structures. Andrea Placidi, the IRC Construction Delegate, identified what has been a key problem for Oxfam:

> ❡ I think it is the inevitable legacy of working here in the war time, that there was little long-term investment. Most NGOs worked on emergency funds, which were limited to the period of the emergency and short-term projects ... Oxfam would have found it a lot easier to push its ideas forward if it had more funds. Trying to influence others is great, and I got a lot of support from Oxfam which influenced my project, but you can't force others to follow your approach, and it's easier to be radical with your own funds. If Oxfam had been able to invest more in local structures, it would have had more power to change them and better co-operation with them now. ❡

In the past, aid agencies worldwide have been criticised for meeting the essential needs of a population in conflict, enabling the government to convert the national budget into a war budget and even financially benefit from the aid effort. In Bosnia, where many industries are State-controlled, aid and development agencies are widely seen as a source of funds. Buying winter-relief clothing in a State factory brings in a good income for the State, especially where workers' salaries have not been paid for many months. But aid agencies can be seen as posing a threat to the State — when promoting NGO development, for example. Not all governments welcome the idea of an independent sector monitoring their performance. Like many other governments, Bosnia's central authorities would like to control the NGO sector. There is a real danger here of producing what has been termed GONGOs: government-organised non-government organisations!

Oxfam in Bosnia seems generally to have been perceived as having a radical approach — too radical for some people. Just as adult female employees who object to being referred to as 'girls' are seen as radical feminists, Oxfam's insistence on supporting the rights of disabled people was considered extreme by some. This radical approach may have sometimes been counter-productive, and compromise might have been more effective in the long term. An example is Oxfam's attempts to get other agencies opening new centres or buildings to make them wheelchair-accessible. The typical response — that the project in question was not a disability project, but for teenagers, the elderly, women etc. — arises from the common tendency in aid agencies to pigeon-hole target groups into separate and isolated categories. Women's projects rarely meet the needs of all women; youth centres rarely cater for the needs of disabled youths. The additional costs of changing an existing plan or project were most commonly cited as the reasons for not making buildings accessible to wheelchairs, even though accessibility incorporated at the planning stage is very cheap, compared with the costs of later adaptation. Oxfam staff were most effective in influencing changes in other agencies through personal connections, where the codes of friendship imposed obligations to look for compromise solutions.

It is clear that Bosnia is in a period of transition and that attitudes are changing, some quicker than others. The process is just beginning. Disabled people themselves are starting to question, to protest, and to develop a very different vision of the future. One visible change has been among the professionals actually working in the Koraci Nade Centre, who are seeing the results of a very different approach. Direct experience of a different way of working, although undoubtedly difficult at first, has been much more powerful than any theory. While there is a long way to go yet, and, for a variety of reasons, some of those in policy-making positions are very reticent about the need for change, Oxfam's focus on community development has had very visible results. However the problems caused by lack of constructive contact with the local government and State systems need to be addressed urgently and some repair work must be done if Oxfam is going to be really effective in supporting a new approach in Bosnia.

As the political system moves towards multi-party democracy, a strong NGO sector is needed. This will necessitate a review of the relationship between the State and the individual. Bosnia has been irreversibly changed by four years of destruction and conflict, and massive international intervention. In the future a new system that allows a 'bottom-up' rather than 'top-down' approach needs to be strengthened. The first step is to promote awareness among the community that they have not only the power to bring about change, but also the right to do so. The gradual development of a democratic multi-party system will produce not only an emerging NGO sector, but also increased competition between political parties, and the growth of accountability. The future government of Bosnia will not simply give the populace a voice: the populace will have to demand it as their right and use the opportunities of a new system to their benefit.

The next chapter will look at how the intervention of aid agencies has affected disabled people and the development of a disability movement, and the methods which will enable people with a vision for change to turn that vision into a reality.

above More than 250,000 people were killed during the war, and thousands more were disabled.

Disability and conflict

6

War as an opportunity for change

By early 1994, Oxfam staff had not only analysed the problems of disabled people in Bosnia, but had also identified the opportunities which the war would open up, as this extract from a report by Lisa Gilliam, Deputy Country Representative in May 1994, illustrates:

> ❧ As dreadful as the situation is, it presents an incredible opportunity for social change. Institutions and services have collapsed and people are looking to the outside for answers. Tuzla is now open to alternative ways of thinking, and disabled people stand to benefit greatly if they can mobilise themselves. When the war ends, this opportunity may be lost as the State reverts in full force to the old approach ... various new institutions will certainly be built as soon as there is enough money. Any attempt by disabled people to create a voice for themselves would probably be seen as a threat to the system that has always 'taken care of disabled people very well'. ❧

Perhaps the very social changes that occur in a time of conflict are actually conducive to the introduction of radical new ways of thinking. Fiona Gell, Adviser on Gender and Social Development in Oxfam's Emergencies Department, poses the question:

> ❧ It seems that it is not only possible to work on social development projects in an unstable society, but also that unstable societies sometimes provide the necessary conditions of shift and change to allow the adoption of new models, such as the social model of disability. The emergence of women into the public and political area in many situations of conflict around the world is a similar process, with traditional norms breaking down and giving way to progressive alternatives. As Oxfam's disability and development programmes in Eastern Europe have in the main grown from roots in crisis and disaster,

it is perhaps worth considering what the challenges would be when trying to introduce such a model in an Eastern European country which has not been racked by war and devastation. Is the chaos of conflict a necessary catalyst for achieving this kind of social change in post-communist states? **⁊**

This casebook cannot answer the question, but I would venture the view that it is certainly unlikely that such a rapid development of the social model of disability would have happened in Bosnia without the war. Complex factors were at work: the massive international presence in Bosnia, the funds and resources allocated to the humanitarian aid effort, the disintegration of the existing system and the number of professionals who left Bosnia during the war, leaving the way open for students and para/non-professionals to become more involved in rehabilitation and disability work. For the majority of the population, the experience of having to rely on their own resources rather than a welfare state in order to survive during the war has also undoubtedly strengthened community and grassroots initiatives. Another factor is that some of the parents at the Koraci Nade Centre felt that, given the exigencies of the war, they had no other option than Koraci Nade; even if they disagreed with its working methods, they regarded it as better than having no facilities at all. This gave the Centre time to prove its working methods to parents who otherwise might not have become involved. During the war, Koraci Nade may have been seen as just an emergency stop-gap, particularly because of its low-technology approach. Indeed, it has only been since the peace agreement that both staff and parents have really started to consider its working methods as a new approach for the future.

After her 1994 visit, Helen Lee also outlined the role that Oxfam could play in supporting associations of disabled people in the future:

> **❻** I think that Oxfam has a role in supporting and strengthening associations of disabled people so that they can develop a stronger voice in society to influence change. Ideas such as the workshops to train people in assertiveness and lobbying skills would be part of this process. Attending seminars and conferences to share experience and ideas with other disabled people on relevant issues such as independent living options would also be important, at a time when more institutions are being considered by policy makers. **⁊**

Since then the situation in Bosnia has improved dramatically, and the movement towards a multi-party democracy has begun, which will offer many more opportunities for organisations of disabled people to campaign and do advocacy work, and to monitor the performance of government. But this will be possible only if disabled people can come together and co-operate more. However, just as the war in Bosnia has not followed its own course in isolation from the influences of the international community, so the disability community in Bosnia has been affected by the interventions of agencies such as Oxfam.

Charity or change?

But what of the organisations which have not received support from international agencies? Associations of disabled people in Bosnia, some of them in existence for 50 years or more, are generally finding it difficult to make the transition from their role as part of the State system in the pre-war period to their new roles as independent sustainable organisations. Their funding had been provided mainly by the State-controlled national lottery, but as Yugoslavia broke up, so did the national lotteries, and funding stopped. Now the priorities of international donors mean that groups focusing on human rights, income generation, and skills training are much more likely to receive funding and support than more traditional associations which still exemplify the charitable approach. The former system was designed to deliver welfare benefits to individuals, rather than radical change to society in general. In order to adapt, the associations have to become organisations which promote change. The war has further compounded their problems, because so many of them had to focus on supplying immediate needs for survival, and are surrounded by foreign relief-orientated NGOs as models from elsewhere in the world.

Some of the more traditional associations are backing away from the rights-based advocacy approach of newer organisations such as the Centre for Self-Reliance (described later in this chapter), or the Association of Mothers. At a time when Bosnia is changing very rapidly, there are some who seek refuge in the past, in the hope that the former system will be revived — because it was at least familiar, and for many it offered power and status. By not working with the newer and more progressive organisations, the leaders of traditional associations have become increasingly alienated from the new approach promoted by the international community. The president of one organisation in Tuzla, evidently feeling very threatened by recent changes, tried to ban his members from attending the Lotos Centre for fear that it would dissipate his power and authority.

It seems clear that those unwilling to adapt will be left behind, but in discussions on this subject most people seem to feel that they have a choice:

'Come and face the future with us or stay at home and dream of a past which is never coming back.' Increasingly it is the young people of Bosnia who are likely to be the new leaders of a disability movement, and it is those very people who are talking of using the InterNet, computer and foreign-language training, advocacy, and changing social attitudes. War-disabled (mainly) young men want all the opportunities they had before the war, and are not disabled by years of institutions and a system which told them that they had no rights. Where war-disabled and pre-war disabled people can come together, they will undoubtedly be stronger, but they will also have to ensure that a cross-disability movement does meet the needs of the most isolated and vulnerable disabled people — people with learning difficulties, people who do not communicate in the conventional way, people with the most severe impairments.

Koraci Nade: a catalyst for change

The Koraci Nade Centre has managed to combine the old and new approaches to disability, by meeting immediate needs and providing a service for disabled children, and by encouraging a new approach, based on human rights, among rehabilitation professionals. The centre has had a great influence on its staff members, many of whom are teachers in the Faculty of Defectology, who send their students to the Centre for practical training.

Koraci Nade has also brought parents together. Koraci Nade staff acknowledge that they have lacked the time and resources to offer much support to parents, but ironically the parents may have benefited from this in the long term. The Association of Mothers was started by a group of parents who were dissatisfied with the lack of support they got from the Koraci Nade Centre. The Association now plays a very political role, and is focused on campaigning for human rights and better services for disabled children. Had Oxfam funded a counsellor or psychologist to work with parents in Koraci Nade, as was requested on several occasions, the parents would probably not have emerged as such a strong force with so much potential to bring about future change.

The Association meets in the Lotos Centre, thus bringing together disabled adults and parents of severely disabled children. Unfortunately, when Koraci Nade was originally set up, Oxfam did not have links with disabled adults who could be involved in the management of the Centre. At the time, the associations of disabled people were very preoccupied with meeting immediate relief needs. The next step will be to bring together rehabilitation professionals and disabled adults, and to give disabled adults influence in defining services for disabled children. The lack of involvement of disabled adults in key positions in the Koraci Nade Centre also means that there are few disabled adults to act as role-models for the children in the Centre. Children attending the Lotos Centre do have opportunities to interact with disabled adults, who are very much in control of their own environment.

Relations between military and civilian groups of disabled people

During the war in Bosnia, people disabled before the war received very little support from the medical structures or the social services. Even as these structures have begun to improve during peace-time, pre-war disabled people remain at the bottom of the agenda. The government estimates that there were about 12,000 disabled people in Bosnia before the war, and that between 40,000 and 70,000 people became disabled during the war. There is no independent verification of these figures, and the huge disparity between 40,000 and 70,000 makes the statistic useless. One should always be aware that statistics concerning people killed and permanently disabled on each side have often been exaggerated as part of the propaganda of war. We can assume, though, that large numbers of soldiers were seriously injured and that many of them have become permanently disabled. Civilian areas came under heavy shell fire during the war, and large numbers of civilians must have been

below Emil Razvaliac (25) was a waiter in a cafe before the war. He was injured in Srebrenica by a shell which killed two of his friends.

Oxfam/Bill Stephenson

permanently disabled by shelling, sniper fire, and landmines. Apart from war-related injuries, car accidents were a serious danger during the war. Other people will have become disabled through other kinds of accidents, and at least the same number of children will have been born with congenital impairments as in the pre-war period. The breakdown of the medical services will also have left more people disabled through lack of appropriate medical attention than in the pre-war period.

Despite the large number of disabled people, and the variety of causes of disability, the government has supported only one association for disabled people: the Association of Disabled War Veterans. All disabled people who have been through the process of 'categorisation' — which assesses their precise degree of disability — are entitled to a disability pension proportional to the severity of their impairment; but when I carried out interviews in November 1996, I learned that this pension had not been paid since the previous May.

The Association of Disabled War Veterans has much closer links with the government and is resented by some other groups of disabled people, who feel that their own needs have been neglected. In 1995 Oxfam started to work with this association. At the time it was the only group which was actually taking action on rights issues for disabled people. A report written by Usha Kar, Oxfam's Country Representative from October 1994 to October 1996, illustrated why Oxfam felt it was important to work with the War Veterans at that time:

> ❝ We should be working with both pre-war and war-disabled people. The war-disabled currently have more political power; pre-war disabled are extremely vulnerable, and unless war-disabled people begin to articulate and demand their rights, in the long term they will become as vulnerable and unsupported as the pre-war disabled people. Therefore the long-term interests of both groups may well be better served by a united voice. ❞

I spoke to Dzevad Junuzovic, a representative of the Association of Disabled War Veterans, about the work of the association and what it had achieved since its first contact with Oxfam. He told me:

> ❝ War-disabled people are still in a very difficult position: they have a lot of problems, especially with housing. I don't think that war-disabled people's rights are protected in law, but this association is very strong and we intend to fight for our rights. War-disabled people get the same government support as other disabled people, but their pensions haven't been paid since May. We don't get much support from international aid organisations, perhaps because they assume that the

government is giving us everything, and that we are a military organisation. Oxfam has given us clothing and some rubber parts for crutches; we are very grateful for that. Our members are not professional soldiers: they didn't choose to go into the army, they were mobilised. They're certainly not in the army now! We have 1,500 members, but we are expecting more as people go through their categorisation tests. We are the municipal association, and there is a cantonal association, and then the national association in Sarajevo. Legal issues for war-disabled people are represented in Sarajevo, but we work on other issues locally. We are trying to influence new laws, and the government has asked our association to make a plan. We've done that, but the government doesn't have the money to implement the plan.

In terms of being political, this election was a new thing for us. The elections were supposed to be democratic, but we had to vote for the nationalist parties. We couldn't choose the party we thought would do the most for disabled people, which is probably the Liberal Party. We couldn't afford to spread out the vote among various parties, because that would have left us in a weaker position compared with the Serb and Croat parties. In the long term the multi-party system should give us more rights, but for now we don't really care who is at the top — we just want more support. Now we have to try and change the nationalist party to be more democratic. We are not a nationalist organisation: we have members from all ethnic groups, we help Serbs and Croats as well as Muslims. We also have contacts with the equivalent association in the Serb entity; we want to have closer contact and more co-operation with them in the future. Like us, they didn't choose to fight: 90 per cent of them were mobilised.

We would like to try and change the ruling party, but the election was the first after the war and people were still in the war mentality. We were afraid of the consequences of not voting for the SDA. The multi-party system hasn't really got working yet. It wasn't a very good time for an election — the influence of other countries is too high in Bosnia.

We are optimistic that war-disabled people will get more rights in future, and that this organisation will become stronger and stronger. You're right that the Vietnam Veterans were strong in America, but how long did it take them? And they didn't have the effects of a war in their own country! We will need a lot longer. There isn't really a disability movement in Bosnia. We don't really spend much time with other associations, we don't have time. There are just too many people to deal with. There are too many problems, like today a man came to see me because he needs money to get married.

> However, we do have our own company, called 'The 13th March', which employs disabled war veterans. It was started by war-disabled people and makes monuments to those who died in the war. Six war-injured people work there. We have lots of plans. We also send war-injured people to other countries for medical treatment, and co-operate with doctors in other countries. This is what we use our funds for mainly. **⁊**

While the association has become much stronger politically, it has not so far made links with other groups of disabled people, and does not attempt to represent their needs and rights. Even though the situation of war veterans is not significantly better than that of pre-war disabled people, the hope of a unified voice to fight for improvements for all disabled people has not been realised. Despite this, all the groups interviewed for this casebook agreed that closer links and co-operation between groups of disabled people were essential in order to increase the power of disabled people and create a disability movement.

Edina Barjaktarevic from the Lotos Centre explains the frustrations of pre-war disabled people and the resentment they feel about the preferential treatment of war veterans:

> **❧** War veterans are treated as though they are heroes and as if they somehow have more rights than the rest of us — for housing, salaries, getting a car and so on. But I wonder what will happen once they get forgotten like the Vietnam veterans? We do have some contact with them, but we know that we need better co-ordination. **⁊**

The Lotos Centre is suffering from the lack of a unified voice for all disabled people. The associations of disabled people in Tuzla have not really embraced the idea of a cross-disability centre, because they are concerned that one association will start to become stronger than the others and take power. The individuals who attend the Lotos Centre have a variety of impairments, and are members of various associations, but the heads of these associations will not endorse Lotos and are worried that it will take over their membership.

Now staff from Lotos are being offered the opportunity to travel and meet other disabled people who are part of a rights-based movement. This is likely to have the most significant impact on the emergence of a disability movement in Bosnia.

An overview of the disability movement in Bosnia

The disability 'movement' in Bosnia is not, as yet, a movement in terms of a united effort to move forward in a common direction, but rather a loose network of associations and groups. However, there is a core group of people who are interested in a cross-disability centre where a co-ordinated effort could be launched to fight for the rights of disabled people. The Centre for Self-Reliance in Sarajevo is a very good example of an association initiated by war-disabled people, but which has already established links with other associations. Its founder, Faruk Sabanovic, does not feel that there is a disability movement in Bosnia yet, but his initiative might just be the catalyst for starting one.

The Centre for Self-Reliance

I went to visit the Centre for Self-Reliance in Sarajevo on its opening day. Faruk told me how the Centre came about, and what it plans to do in the future.

❡ I had been having medical rehabilitation in Bosnia, but was given the chance to go to the USA on an IRC [International Rescue Committee] project with the *New York Times*. After just a month of treatment in the USA, I realised that everything they had told me over here had been wrong. They were just using the same treatment for everybody, when in fact we were all different. In Bosnia they told me I would walk again within six months; in the States I found out that I would never walk again. There I got individual treatment and I met lots of people who were active in the disability movement, and I came up with the idea for the Centre. Everywhere in the States is really accessible too. I spoke to a lot of people about how to set up the Centre and things that I could do, and that really inspired me.

I realise now that my biggest mistake was that I really believed I would walk again after six months, so I just waited for those six months to be over. I made a lot of mistakes and didn't use my time in the USA as I could have done. But when I came back to Bosnia, I made a plan for this Centre and put a proposal to IRC, and they gave me some funding — so that's how it started. The problem was that I wrote the proposal in January and we only opened the Centre in November — everything is so very slow here.

I want this to be a centre based on the InterNet, so we can try to bring the interests of all disabled people in one direction. The Centre will also offer vocational training, and a database of disabled individuals and organisations. We will mainly focus on advocacy, information, and training. We are starting a course in desk-top publishing, some income-generating projects — we want to be self-sustainable, instead of having to rely on outside funding. The trip to America is the reason why this Centre exists. It showed me what the possibilities are. I learned that a miracle will not happen, we have to work to make things for ourselves. I am attending the University here, but it's not accessible for me and it will cost a lot of money to make the adaptations — so I want to start a project so that students can study through e-mail.

There are lots of disabled people and associations, but the problems of accessibility and awareness are common. We have links with different associations, and especially the Cerebral Palsy Association. We want this Centre to be for everyone — to be a place where each person can achieve their vision. At the moment we are working with a lawyer from the Cerebral Palsy Association who knows about legal issues. We are never consulted on new laws, so we plan to draft some new ideas. We also want to produce posters on advocacy: we are having a competition to design a poster.

This is the first centre of its type in Sarajevo. There is no disability movement in Bosnia. We need to get all the associations to come together. We need to create groups of people for self-reliance. We don't want always to be asking for help. We want to help create laws that will respect our rights. **7**

The Lotos Centre

The Lotos Centre in Tuzla is a project with similar aims to the Centre for Self-Reliance. Kaca Sarihodzic, Oxfam's Programme Assistant, who is responsible for the project, explained the situation for disabled people and what she feels are the problems for disabled people trying to take action together.

6 Before the war this country didn't meet all of its responsibilities to disabled people. In some ways the government was good, in others it wasn't: the country provided medical rehabilitation and institutions and thought that everything was solved by that approach. Disabled people were living separately, with little or no contact with their society. But we cannot totally blame our country for this situation, because we did nothing to change it either: no one fought for the right to go to ordinary school, for example. Maybe a few well-educated disabled people managed to get jobs, mostly those with a mild disability. But adults with cerebral palsy, for example, had no chance. I have a friend in Belgrade, Predrag, who has cerebral palsy and is now a lawyer. But his parents taught him and gave him a lot of opportunities, not the State. He speaks English and can use a computer very well, and has written books about the law, but he can still only get a job with the Union of Disabled People.

Society must learn about what disabled people need and what are the rights of disabled people. There are no disabled people in our government, and we are never consulted on anything important. How do I feel things could change? We must organise ourselves, and I think that this Centre has given us the right opportunity to organise. The problem is that disabled people don't trust each other and we don't communicate well with each other. We also don't make allowances for the physical or communication differences of different disabled people, and also how that makes us the people we are. For example, deaf people have their own separate culture; wheelchair-users focus on problems of access. We just concentrate on our own problems for our own impairment. We need to come together and then we can be strong. Disabled people have the potential to be very influential, but how will the government know what we want if they don't ask us?

I want lots of things from the government: financial independence, social security, pension, and the ability to get work. I want medical support when I need it, and an improvement in the current services, better enabling aids too. I want an accessible home, accessibility for everyone in fact, whatever the barriers are, and I want to have access to education and have influence in public life. If we can get over our internal problems and fight for these things together, then we can be really strong. **7**

Many disabled people and the newer organisations have defined lack of consultation on legislation affecting disabled people as a central issue of concern. In the pre-war period there were some systems in Bosnia for consulting associations of disabled people on legislative issues, but the number of disabled people who have raised the issue illustrates that many disabled people were alienated from the consultation process. Consultation through the associations also cuts out those people who are under-represented in the membership, or who have little power within the associations. In the course of my research for this book, only the Association of Disabled War Veterans stated that they had actually been consulted on legislation affecting disabled people, although it is true that many of the other associations and organisations had been set up in the post-war period and would not necessarily know about pre-war structures.

The new environment in which a Bosnian NGO sector is emerging should give these more radical organisations the means to challenge and influence government in the future. But the first priority is to develop mechanisms for cross-disability representation — a means to bring all disabled people together — and this is not currently happening. In bringing together a diverse group of disabled people, the organisers will have to plan carefully to ensure that all are represented equally. It is concern about this issue that is currently blocking progress. There are other factors which tend to divide disabled people. Ethnic tensions will inevitably prevail after four years of war, but they are more likely to be recognised as real issues than other factors such as sexism, which is considered a lower priority in moves towards the increasing democratisation of associations.

The role of women within the disability movement

The roles of women within organisations of disabled people vary, but they are rarely found in the powerful, decision-making positions. In fact, to an outside visitor, women are most often seen serving coffee while male representatives hold meetings. However, there are exceptions, such as Edina Barjaktarevic, who started the Srebrenik Association of Paraplegics in 1993.

The women's movement itself is, like the disability movement, a fledgling creation, making the transition from relief and war-related priorities to promoting women's rights and political participation. Within the women's movement there are very few active disabled women. The first organisation to take on disability seriously was the Association of Women, who started the support group for mothers of disabled children which inspired the Koraci Nade Centre, but mainly from the point of view of women as carers, rather than promoting the rights of disabled women and girls. Disabled women do not feel that the associations and unions adequately represent their needs, but there are few women who are willing or able to take on a more active role. The main factor they cite as blocking women's involvement in associations is the burden of domestic chores and family duties, which often take a disabled woman much longer to complete, leaving her with little time to get involved in other activities.

Another factor is the disparities which mark the experiences of rural women and urban women. It is true that many Bosnia women are studying and employed in the technical sciences (although not in the highest posts), but they are women from urban areas; the situation for rural women is very different. During a group discussion in the Lotos Resource Centre, one woman told the group that she felt that the situation for disabled women in Bosnia was very good. In response, Kaca Sarihodzic commented:

❧ The situation might seem good from the point of view of a woman who is a wheelchair-user who works in a bank, has an accessible home and lives in a town, but I know a lot of women who don't even get a chance to go to school. They are not even accepted within their families.

In the villages women are much less accepted than men, even more so if they are disabled. Disabled women are hidden away, so they don't affect the marriage chances of their brothers and sisters. **⟩**

Similar discrimination is experienced by disabled girls across many cultures, particularly where women's status and rights are heavily suppressed. In India, for example, disabled girls have much reduced educational opportunities and limited chances of finding marriage partners. Their disability may be considered such a stigma for the whole family that they are hidden or turned out of the house to beg. Many disabled female babies do not even survive. Fortunately there is no evidence of such extreme discrimination in Bosnia, but the double handicap experienced by women and girls who are disabled needs to be recognised.

Another group discussion in the Lotos Centre looked at the general situation for women and girls in Bosnia today, and then compared the situation of disabled women. The women in the group were divided between wanting to emphasise that they were European women who had lived in a relatively liberated way before the war, and looking really critically at the current reality of their lives. There is an element of racism in Bosnian society, especially related to the aid effort. Bosnian people are very sensitive about being perceived as unsophisticated, and wary of how they present themselves to the outside world. The results of the discussions were put on a chart, reproduced in edited form overleaf. It represents how ten individual disabled girls and women define their position, and therefore may not necessarily be how all Bosnian women see their situation.

After the session, the women involved started to define the real needs of disabled women, and particularly the lack of protection for severely disabled women in institutions. The Lotos Centre is carrying out analysis and raising issues, but lacks confidence to move forward into political action and campaigning. This is partly because it is an unfamiliar role for many Bosnian people, and there are no examples of rights campaigns in their country to use as models. There has also been a long tradition of individual people feeling disempowered by the one-party State. The transition to a multi-party democracy will not happen overnight, but it has begun. One woman pointed out: *'The country is like a new-born baby: we are just waiting to see if it is a boy or a girl!'*

	Women in general	Disabled women
health care	Generally good services, although men got priority in war. Many female medical staff, but not in highest positions. Screenings for breast/cervical cancer on request; free contraception and abortion, good ante-natal and post-natal care. Charges imposed for some services — difficult for poor women.	Same rights as non-disabled women in theory, but architectural barriers pose problems, and special needs such as sign interpretation are not met.
education	Equal access to school and university for boys and girls. Equally represented in arts and technical subjects. Many female teachers, fewer directors of schools, and even fewer women in Ministry of Education.	In theory disabled children have the same right to an education, but in reality this is a big problem — not just architectural barriers, but deeply entrenched attitudinal barriers. Children were educated in institutions before the war; now special facilities are in short supply.
employment	Women have equal opportunities and equal pay, but there are not enough women in the top jobs, and child-care is a problem for many women.	In theory disabled women have the same opportunities as other women, but not in reality. A few women with slight impairments are working; no opportunities for others.
economic rights	Women have equal pay and benefits (sick pay, pensions), rights to own and inherit property and land, and the right to control their own bank accounts; but often benefits are not paid. Big problems for single mothers. Equal access to humanitarian aid.	In law disabled and non-disabled women have the same rights, but disability allowance is just a token amount and the reality is that disabled women are in a very difficult situation.
politics	The women's party is not very strong and no one present would vote for it yet. Few women politicians; women's issues are bottom of the political agenda. Active and powerful women's NGOs in Bosnia.	The women's party has some focus on disability. The women's NGOs do not represent needs of disabled women.

	Women in general	**Disabled women**
social status	Women have equal status in society, are equally prominent in all areas. Many Bosnian swear words refer to women's sexuality or bodies. Women at increasing risk of violence in society. More alcoholism among men, more drug abuse among young people.	Disabled girls and women have very low status in society, and are not very prominent on the streets. More at risk from abuse and violence.
effects of war	Many female-headed households. Search for missing men is a big strain on women, as is the threat of rape and sexual violence. Women active in the military, fought at the front line, but not mobilised except for medical staff. No significant anti-war movement in Bosnia.	Disabled girls and women much more vulnerable in war. Many injured by shelling and sniping.
law	The constitution treats women and men equally.	In theory disabled women have the same rights, but they are not upheld or protected.
rural/ urban lives	Rural women's lives are more limited than urban women's. Women marry very young in villages, receive less education, and have fewer opportunities for employment, etc.	Disabled women in rural areas are in the worst situation in terms of all the above.

UNHCR

above A minefield in Ilidza, near Sarajevo. Not all mine-fields in Bosnia are so clearly marked. The task of identifying the sites and defusing the mines will take years.

Development work in a context of conflict 7

One of the most difficult issues for relief agencies such as Oxfam is the relationship between emergency work and long-term developmental work. Within relief agencies there is often an institutional division between emergency-response staff and those working on development projects. Different skills and experience are needed for quick-impact emergency work and long-term development work. Longer-term programmes employ many more local staff; emergency work is dominated by ex-patriates, who have easier freedom of movement and are considered less personally affected by the emergency.

The high media profile of emergencies makes fund-raising relatively easy while the news is hot; but when the attention of the media turns elsewhere, donations from the public start to dry up. Raising funds for longer-term work, less thrilling, with a lower profile, and often without immediate results is increasingly difficult.

When an emergency occurs in an area where there is a long-term programme, existing staff may feel threatened by an influx of emergency-response 'outsiders' invading their territory, sometimes with little regard for local sensitivities. The emergencies staff may feel frustrated by the apparent blocks put in their way by field staff desperate to retain control of 'their' programme. Tensions between emergencies and field staff are commonplace, and destructive both to the programme and to morale.

Any emergency situation, whether arising from a natural disaster or, increasingly often, from armed conflict, demands a response to immediate needs for things like food and shelter; but the longer-term effects of the situation must also be taken into account. The affected population will feel the repercussions for many years to come. In wars, not only are people killed and injured, and homes, communications, roads and bridges destroyed, but also the economy, the social welfare system, education services and the community support system disintegrate. The death or displacement of high-profile community leaders such as politicians, civil servants, doctors and other professionals can leave a country in chaos.

Once the fighting stops, the battle for survival continues, and the needs of the population are not automatically met as soon as the ink dries on a peace agreement. But peace does not always come: Bosnia saw over 30 cease-fires and agreements made in four years — every one broken, some within a matter of hours — before the Dayton Agreement was signed. Even following Dayton, the peace in Bosnia can at best be described as 'uneasy'. Other countries see decades go by with no resolution to a conflict. In such countries, the problems of the population extend beyond basic 'immediate' needs. Only in the most extreme emergencies will a response be governed solely by meeting basic needs for a prolonged period. Generally an emergency response must be closely linked to a longer-term programme, to address the needs of the population beyond the immediate crisis. Conversely it would be useless to try to launch a pure development programme in any situation without first ensuring that basic immediate needs are met.

It is often observed that in critical situations people tend to make great efforts to keep their lives as normal as possible. A measure of the impact of a traumatic event is to watch for the signs of everyday behaviour. Children will play football with screwed-up balls of cardboard; women will make every attempt to wash some clothes, hang up a blanket to air, organise the space around their family. When there are no signs of any attempts to 'normalise' an abnormal situation, then the situation is very desperate indeed.

Clearly, normalising behaviour is a coping strategy, a way in which people deal with traumatic events and their after-effects. This should be seen as a pattern for NGO interventions. School attendance is widely recognised as playing a crucial role in helping children to cope with conflict or disaster; many makeshift schools have operated in basements under shell fire, with children crawling through tunnels each morning and evening. The re-establishment of something akin to a familiar pattern is a crucial part of any response, as we can see with the Koraci Nade Centre and the role it played in establishing a routine for parents and disabled children in the war.

Planning for long-term development

There need be no conflict between immediate emergency responses and long-term development. In fact, we can incorporate planning for the future into much of our emergency work.

In emergency work, aid agencies which plan a quick in/out intervention often get trapped into a longer-term commitment because the very factors which cause or exacerbate an emergency fail to respond to this kind of tactic: they are usually complex factors, which need a more complex response. In Bosnia, survival rations and winter clothing were not reaching disabled people. A quick response could have been an intensive aid distribution, but factors that made these people more vulnerable than others — most especially their social and physical isolation — needed to be addressed in both the immediate crisis and for the period beyond the acute stage of the emergency.

Helen Lee, Oxfam's Disability Adviser, wrote in May 1994:

> ❝ There is a need to strike the right balance between giving practical
> help and the longer-term development process; the former is relatively
> easy, of course, and necessary, but the latter, I feel, should be the priority
> if meaningful change is to happen for disabled people. ❞

In Tuzla, Oxfam has been running both emergency-relief programmes, such
as the distribution of winter clothing, and longer-term projects. Isolated from
Oxfam's traditional expertise in the provision of clean water, safe shelter, and
tools and seeds for self-sufficiency, the Oxfam Tuzla programme was managed at
the field level by staff new to Oxfam, who were unfamiliar with the Emergencies
Department and unaware of what resources were available to them in terms of
emergency personnel and stocks of relief items. Apart from relief work, Oxfam's
programme in Bosnia was centred on work with women — and projects with
disabled people. The women's workshops initially provided a space in collective
centres where women could gather together and knit relief items for distribution by
Oxfam. In the winter of 1994 the project registered as a local NGO — BOSFAM.
Within a year, many displaced people had been moved out of collective centres
and BOSFAM was developing a longer-term strategy concerned with the tracing of
missing people and the promotion of women's rights in the future Bosnia.
Work with disabled people was not able to move from immediate interventions to longer-term goals so quickly — and this reflects the way in which
disabled people were generally excluded from the international aid effort, and
the fact that their general situation was much worse than that of other groups.

below An Oxfam-funded workshop in Solina, Tuzla, for women refugees.

Oxfam/Mike Goldwater

The need for a flexible response

During any emergency, especially a complex political crisis, needs will change very rapidly and it will be difficult to make exact predictions, although some general assumptions can be made. The strength of Oxfam in Bosnia was its range of flexible projects for responding to different aspects of disability, some of which have had differing profiles during the war. The urgent needs of disabled children were the initial main priority of the Koraci Nade Centre, while the priority now is probably to support their parents' role and to strengthen them and other groups in their efforts to put pressure on the government to take responsibility for the needs of the children. The ZID workshop is also playing a crucial role. It did not manage to fulfil its potential until the beginning of 1996, because buying materials and tools was very difficult before then; now the workshop is in the process of deciding whether to register as an NGO in order to get international funding to continue producing enabling aids until a time when the State will provide them. This might mean that ZID gradually starts to change its focus, if other more sustainable sources of aids become available, or it may become part of the State structure in the long term. The key to all these projects is maintaining the flexibility to be able to adapt to changing needs and to emphasise different aspects of a programme at appropriate times. A range of different projects and actions makes up a programme; some can be kept on hold until the conditions allow, while others will be phased out when they are no longer appropriate. Strategic planning is an ideal way to plan for project flexibility and to develop an approach composed of a variety of projects or actions, designed to meet both immediate needs and predicted needs.

From the experience of the Tuzla Oxfam office and the Koraci Nade project during the war in Bosnia, we can learn about some of the main issues that concern NGOs working in conflict. Some of them relate directly to the fighting; others are side-effects of the conflict, and it is these which are often overlooked or not planned for: the mobilisation of key members of staff, and the problem of providing salaries and support for professional staff, for example.

Funding and legal status

One issue of concern which spanned the war and post-war period in Bosnia is funding. For many months, Bosnia was on the world's TV screens and in the headlines almost every day. Events such as the taking of Srebrenica by the Bosnian Serb Army in July 1995 prompted large donations of money from the British public, which were used to finance emergency work and longer-term work in the region. After the war, investment in large-scale reconstruction work (financed mainly by the World Bank and European Union) is complemented by financial support for local NGOs, which have been prioritised for field-level funding. As elsewhere, this tendency to prioritise local NGOs has resulted in the appearance of an increasing number of associations with access to large grants, but without appropriate skills in NGO management, representation and democratic structures, financial accountability, and so on. Without doubt, the local NGO community in Bosnia is very strongly donor-led, and unsustainable without the presence of international donor agencies. In the short term, one of the results of this policy is that small-scale initiatives are moulded to match donors' requirements. Local NGOs receive little support in terms of skills-training and are not accountable to their memberships.

As we have seen, for the Koraci Nade staff the prospect of becoming a local NGO was much more attractive than the option of becoming part of the local State structure. For Oxfam, it would be quicker and less bureaucratic to register the project as a local NGO, so it has been a challenge to keep trying to negotiate a solution with the local authorities, rather than just to select the easiest option. However, the current trends in funding in Bosnia are likely to make it harder and harder for this kind of initiative to survive much longer.

One of the reasons why Koraci Nade staff were concerned about being absorbed into the local authorities was that most of them are totally dependent on their Oxfam pay packets. It is true that they have been on short-term contracts which did not offer any security, but during the war few people were making long-term plans anyway. Now as their former places of work start to open up again, staff have to make a choice: carry on working at the centre, taking a chance that it will provide them with continuing employment, or return to their State jobs, which offer much lower pay initially, but perhaps better security in the long term. In a country where the job-for-life offered considerable security and benefits, this is a very difficult choice. Another option for some of the staff is to work on projects of other aid agencies which can guarantee a salary for longer than Oxfam can. The financial benefits of working for an international agency have been a lifeline for many people during the war, and the additional benefits of freedom of movement, UN identity passes, status, contacts, foreign travel for seminars or training courses, and so on made it a very good option during the war.

Retaining professional staff

One of the problems which Oxfam encountered with the original proposal for the Centre from the Association of Women in 1994 was the number of staff they wanted to employ. There is often pressure on project co-ordinators to employ their family and friends, but, as Ajsa Mahmugtagic from the Centre points out, there was a logic behind their ideas during the war.

> ❝ We wanted to show support for professionals during the war, because no one was being paid and it was important to encourage professionals not to leave the country. By having job-shares they could have balanced paid work for Oxfam with unpaid work for the State. Like teachers, most professionals just received an occasional aid packet, and they never knew when it would come or what would be inside. ❞

In fact, in Sarajevo an Oxfam-funded project employed medical staff on an outreach service for war-injured children. One of the benefits of paying a decent salary to medical professionals would be to encourage them to stay in the city, which was desperately short of medical staff. But there has to be a balance between trying to encourage professionals to stay in an area of conflict or other disaster — a role that an aid agency can easily play — and running a workable project which provides a reliable and consistent service. In some countries doctors, nurses, and other medical staff have left their jobs to become drivers and warehouse workers for aid agencies, because they desperately needed the money to survive. There are two ways in which an aid agency can help to support professionals: by offering part-time employment that enables them to carry out their State duties in addition to earning some money to support their families; or by ensuring that they are targeted in relief assistance, as essential service-providers for the community. Doctors and nurses might not be in the most desperate position, but they are the ones who will find it easiest to leave, with a marketable skill they can use in other countries; if encouraged to stay in the area, they will continue to serve the most vulnerable and desperate people.

In the case of Koraci Nade, it should be said that Oxfam did not employ a large number of professional personnel. The agency was trying to change the way in which specialist staff operated, and to challenge the dominance of professional medical personnel in rehabilitation work with disabled people. Maintaining a balance of qualified professionals, students, and non-professionals was an essential part of Oxfam's new approach, which focused on the role of the family and community in rehabilitation. It is debatable whether the same effect could have been achieved, and the same focus on empowerment of parents in the rehabilitation process, with a larger professional team.

Insecurity and danger

Apart from the secondary effects of any emergency — economic issues, breakdown of the social support system and so on — there are also the direct threats such as shelling and sniper-fire and unmarked minefields. The Koraci Nade Centre opened while Tuzla was being regularly shelled, and continued to operate under shell-fire for 18 months. For some of this time the Centre was forced to close, although the outreach visits continued whenever possible. At times shells were landing so close to the Centre that the windows actually cracked, and people were killed by shrapnel just metres away. Cimeta Hatibovic describes the concerns of the staff about security:

> ❜ Of course, we were worried that a shell could hit the Centre. Sometimes I felt under incredible pressure, because I would blame myself if anyone was hurt. In May 1995 I was especially afraid that something could happen, but the mothers still came and still wanted the centre to be open. Really no one knew what could happen — sometimes there was shelling three or four times a day, sometimes a month would go by and nothing — no one knew. When the shelling started, we would go into the hallway, which was a safer place; only once did we go into the cellar, which was actually a café. But when the shelling was really heavy, we closed the Centre and went to visit people in their homes. We went to all the families we could, but it was very dangerous to go out. But the families really wanted us to go and visit, and it was important that they knew that someone cared about them. We used to take some things for the children and some donations that we could get for the parents too. ❜

The shelling of Tuzla was so sporadic and unpredictable that all offices and businesses which were able to work did so; but at one time Tuzla was shelled hourly on the hour, which created a bizarre situation where everyone carried on as normal until five minutes to the hour, when they would take shelter, wait for the shells to land, and then carry on again as before. At other times NATO air-strikes would prompt shelling. External political events, religious holidays, and even the results of sports contests involving teams from the region could be catalysts for renewed action across the front lines. The key indicator used by Oxfam for deciding when to open the Centre was whether regular schools were open. When the government closed State schools, the Centre was always closed as well. When the Centre was closed, parents who lived close to each other were encouraged to gather and form 'mini groups' in their homes, to ensure that the benefits of the social contact for both parents and children were not lost at a time when they were most needed. This pattern was followed with other projects, such as the BOSFAM workshops, which adapted to heavy shelling in some areas by visiting women and taking wool and needles to them, to enable them to continue knitting relief items. However, a workshop in Gracanica, an area which had always been heavily shelled, suffered a direct hit by three shells and was totally destroyed; the women had left just ten minutes earlier. The Kosta Popov School also sent teachers out to areas around Tuzla to gather together small groups of pupils to try and continue their education, although this initiative suffered from lack of transport and a shortage of teachers.

Not only did the Koraci Nade staff feel responsible for the safety of those in the Centre, but they were under the same stress as other people in the town. In particular they worried about the safety of their families. Cimeta Hatibovic recalls:

> ❡ Both my sons were in the army. All the staff were worried about someone in the army — that was the most stressful thing, just to wait and hope everything would be OK. We were all worried about someone — no one was relaxed. Now you can see the effects on the people: they have heart attacks, strokes, high blood pressure. The parents at the Centre were in the same situation. It was important for the mothers to come, so they could spend time with each other, talking about the situation and their problems. They were supporting each other, not just their children. ❡

On 25 May 1995 a single shell hit a square known as the Kapija, a popular gathering place of young people in Tuzla, and 71 teenagers and young people were killed in a single night. The incident left Tuzla in shock. Oxfam staff spent the evening trying to locate their own families and friends, desperately watching television footage of scenes at the hospital to identify clothing or shoes. For days the centre of Tuzla smelt like an abattoir. Nobody could fail to be affected by the event, and many Oxfam office and project staff had friends and relatives killed or injured. Following this incident were several days of very heavy shelling, and schools and public gathering places in Tuzla were closed for much of the summer.

That summer saw one other event that had a huge effect on Tuzla, the repercussions of which are still being felt today. On 11 July the 'safe haven' of Srebrenica in eastern Bosnia was taken by the Bosnian Serb Forces. Thousands of Bosnian Muslims from surrounding villages who were sheltering in the city under almost constant shell-fire began a difficult journey to Tuzla. Men and women were separated — men and boys being kept behind for 'questioning', while women and children were taken by bus to an area several kilometres from the front line and then walked to a reception point on the Bosnian government side. At this point the aid effort began, with the provision of shelter, blankets, and food, before the displaced were taken by bus to Tuzla. In total over 34,000 people arrived in Tuzla. A refugee camp was set up alongside the airport runway, with about 7,000 people accommodated in tents still within range of the Bosnian Serb artillery, desperately wondering what was happening to their male relatives, many of whom, it is now known, were being executed and buried in mass graves.

Oxfam played many different roles in the subsequent aid effort: from assisting amputees to collect water, providing urgent supplies to the hundreds of young babies, and distributing children's shoes to the entire camp at the airport. Oxfam staff were very concerned about the situation of disabled people during the exodus. They carried out a survey of the whole airbase camp, trying to locate disabled people who needed special assistance or equipment such as crutches. The Koraci Nade staff joined Oxfam's field staff in identifying children and adults who should have priority for transfer to more suitable conditions. The Koraci Nade staff made links with the parents of disabled children who could come to the Centre in the future. However, priority was given to immediate needs, such as access to water supplies, and distribution of food and blankets. Later on Koraci Nade staff were able to follow up some disabled children who arrived from Srebrenica and invite them to attend the Centre.

below July 1995: 7,000 of the people forced out of the 'safe haven' of Srebrenica took refuge in a camp at Tuzla airport.

Oxfam/Mike Goldwater

All through the war, male members of staff risked mobilisation into the army. Each time there was a push on mobilisation, Oxfam staff visited the Ministry of Defence to ask that their key staff be spared, to ensure that the aid effort could continue. Each time no promises were made. In certain areas young men were picked up off the streets or collected from their homes. Some of them started to rotate between friends and relatives, sleeping in a different place each night. During the day, fear of being called up and sent to the front line made it difficult for them to concentrate on their work. As a contingency Oxfam employed extra logistics staff who were exempt from mobilisation, and tried its best to support those who lived under the stress of being taken away in the night.

Communications and transport

At the height of the war, Bosnian civilians were cut off from the outside world. Cimeta Hatibovic remembers:

> For all of 1992 and 1993 I couldn't even telephone my mother, who lives just 40 km away — and there was no way I could go and visit her. We couldn't phone people, there was no post, nothing. We didn't have contact with anyone else outside either personally or professionally. We just had the Oxfam office to communicate with the rest of the world.

Long-distance journeys were unthinkable. Even aid agencies travelled in convoys of at least two or three vehicles. Accidents were common, and during the winter the mountain track out of Tuzla was snow-covered for months. Sometimes the journey out of Bosnia took up to two days, as all vehicles had to arrive in a safe location, preferably before nightfall, and certainly before curfew, which was usually between 8 and 9 pm. Aid agency staff were not armed; but, travelling in good-quality four-wheel drive vehicles and often carrying cash from bank accounts held in Croatia, their convoys became a prime target when parked and empty. They could be hi-jacked when stopped in the road at gunpoint; driver and passengers would be ordered out, and the vehicle and all its contents would be stolen.

The difficulties of travel in the region also meant that resources which could not be purchased in Tuzla were difficult to obtain. Koraci Nade Centre lacked equipment, toys, and specialised physiotherapy aids for much of the war; the Faculty of Defectology still has very few books. Not only were resources hard to come by; even when they were delivered from abroad to the Split logistics base, or bought in Croatia, customs procedures were extremely difficult. The Croat-controlled part of Bosnia had declared itself a separate State, Herzog Bosna, with its own customs demands. Usually Herzog Bosna customs tried to claim one third of relief goods for the Croat-dominated region of Hercegovina. With poor communications Oxfam relied on a regular mail pack from the UK, but this could be delivered no nearer than Split, and to collect it took two vehicles and drivers a three-day return trip. Getting information in and out of Bosnia was notoriously difficult.

Competition for national resources

Perhaps the most far-reaching effect of the war on Bosnian society is the way that it has affected government priorities and service-provision. The reconstruction process has begun in the Federation entity, but there are still serious delays in the Republika Srpska, which are causing many problems for the most vulnerable people. During the war all sides saw their governments operating on a crisis agenda. Almost all resources were diverted to the military effort. The aid effort assisted displaced people more than local people, who may have been living in equally difficult circumstances. Priority for medical services was given first to soldiers, and second to war-injured civilians; last in line came the rest of the population. Service-provision for needs unrelated to the war has been very badly affected and is unlikely to improve significantly in the future. While disabled children in Yugoslavia had access to a range of facilities before the war, Bosnian children are now mainly restricted to those in Bosnia itself. The links between parts of the previous system which are now in separate countries are a casualty of the nationalist agendas adopted by all the countries. Some personal linking has gone on, however.

Reconstruction is a highly politicised and contentious matter. In the ten months following the peace agreement, the reconstruction agenda in the Federation entity was informed by the need for the ruling SDA party to be seen to be taking Bosnia into the future. High-profile and vote-winning projects were given priority. Unfortunately disabled people are not a government priority and are unlikely to be so for a long time, although there are some efforts to appoint disabled war veterans to government jobs. The war in Bosnia made already vulnerable disabled people even more vulnerable, and the negative effects of the war did not suddenly disappear when the Dayton Accords were signed, or when the first post-war elections were held. The effects of this war will be felt for a long time before Bosnia starts to recover. First to recover will be the fittest and most able. Disabled people will need much longer, and special support in the process. This book has argued that they will not get this support unless they organise to demand it.

Oxfam/Howard Davies

above Creative play for a mixed group of disabled and non-disabled children at the Koraci Nade Centre.

In conclusion: some lessons for development agencies

8

This casebook tells the story of one Oxfam field office and one particular project. While some of the issues raised are specific to this experience and to local work in Bosnia, others are more broadly relevant. The purpose of recording what happened in Tuzla is to share the lessons learnt with colleagues within Oxfam, but also to draw conclusions and make recommendations which might be useful to other development workers and organisations, including donor organisations.

Why work with disabled people?

During the war everyone in Bosnia was vulnerable to the effects of the conflict: shelling, land-mines, sniping, and sanctions are indiscriminate in their effects. With limited resources, aid and development agencies such as Oxfam were faced with tough choices when deciding, within the scope of their organisational mandate, which groups to work with and how to maximise the impact of their programmes. Agencies have to conduct an analysis and identify those people most vulnerable to poverty and suffering, and those interventions which will make sustainable impacts on poverty.

To do this, Oxfam employs a strategic planning process, whereby the external environment and the internal organisational environment are analysed in terms of strengths, weaknesses, opportunities, and threats. Current trends are then identified, in an attempt to predict the situation in five years' time and to identify who will be most vulnerable. This process helps field offices to give priority for assistance, within their capacity, to those worst-affected by poverty and insecurity.

In any society, at war or in peace, such an analysis is likely to prioritise disabled people. This does not imply that all disabled people are vulnerable, poor, and in need of assistance. Automatic assumptions that all disabled people are necessarily or inevitably vulnerable and unable to reach their full potential deny their many achievements in the face of multiple obstacles. At the same time, even in rich societies, disabled people are unlikely to have equal access to transport, education, jobs, public and private buildings, and so on.

In a crisis, as in Bosnia during the war, the environment becomes even more disabling; everyone is affected, but there is a disproportionate impact on disabled people. In Bosnia, as physical conditions deteriorated, along with welfare and social services, infrastructure, and job opportunities, people become increasingly dependent on their own physical abilities for survival. Flight from danger was especially difficult for disabled people and their carers; living in hastily adapted collective centres was especially arduous for them. Pre-war institutionalised systems of care broke down and were not replaced with resources to support community-based services.

Working with disabled people was identified as an absolute priority for Oxfam in Bosnia. It was recognised that the short- and long-term interests of disabled people are inseparable from the interests of all people. Disability, rather than being a marginal factor affecting a small group of people born with physical impairments, is likely to affect everybody directly at some time in their lives — as carers for disabled people or as disabled people themselves — either temporarily or permanently, following accident or illness or as part of the ageing process. Moreover, society as a whole is the poorer if disabled people are prevented from making a full contribution to the community.

The relevance of disability to everyone's lives is more central in war, given the increased physical vulnerability of the whole population. It is ironic, therefore, that at times of armed conflict some non-disabled aid-agency staff and government officials who control resources are even more likely to regard disability as a marginal issue which affects only a minority of people. There is no good reason for agencies not to insist on a high priority for disability issues on their own and others' agendas.

Human rights and development

Oxfam's approach to all its work around the world is based on the conviction that every person has a basic right to subsistence and security: to a livelihood, a home, an education, health care, a safe environment, protection from violence, equality of opportunity, and a chance to determine his or her future. These rights are enshrined in the Universal Declaration of Human Rights, adopted by the UN General Assembly in 1948.

The strength of this approach is that rights apply to all people equally and objectively. In situations where, as in Bosnia, all people are vulnerable in some way, the approach justifies the prioritisation of those with the least chance of attaining their basic rights, both immediately and in longer-term projections. This may lead to the prioritisation of broadly defined groups of people, such as 'disabled people', but also allows for the fact that not all people within those groups are equally or necessarily poor and vulnerable.

When certain proposed interventions are under discussion, such as the construction of ramps for wheelchair-users, it is all too common to hear arguments against them 'justified' on economic grounds. But a rights-based policy renders such arguments redundant. Denying the right of some people to services, information, and employment to which others have access is as unacceptable as denying the right of a nursing mother to extra nourishment on the basis of cost.

The need for a 'disability analysis'

In most societies, taking a rights-based approach and conducting a vulnerability analysis means that working with disabled people at some level will be inevitable — given the multiple barriers (both attitudinal and environmental) which prevent them from claiming their rights.

As Oxfam did in Bosnia, a development agency may decide that an appropriate response is to work intensively with certain groups of disabled people or to fund disabled people's organisations. But Oxfam also realised that a 'disability analysis' needs to be applied at all levels of *any* programme of intervention, not merely to specialist projects. This is important for several reasons:

- to ensure that disabled people are involved in, not excluded from, programmes;
- to ensure that programmes do not further disadvantage and marginalise disabled people;
- to help disabled people to assert their rights;
- to ensure that society as a whole can benefit from the active participation of those disabled people who are currently marginalised and excluded.

For example, any programme of education held in inaccessible premises and advertised in inaccessible places not only excludes disabled people from the benefits of attendance, but further marginalises them by denying them an equal opportunity in the competition for employment. It also denies other participants in the programme the benefits of the knowledge and experience of the disabled person.

It is important for agencies not only to identify structures which marginalise disabled people but also to ensure that their programmes identify, consult, and involve them. This means considering, for example, not only how a relief distribution is organised but how it is advertised; before this, it means identifying who and where disabled people are, and how to reach and include them. Distributions of food and clothes conducted by throwing items from the back of a truck (as televised at Tuzla air-base after the mass displacement from Srebrenica) not only cause chaos; they are inequitable and an offence against dignity, and they totally exclude disabled people, elderly people, ill people, or anyone else unable to compete physically with others. In addition, they create or reinforce the dependence of those people on more physically able members of their community.

Without a disability analysis, an agency should perhaps consider whether it can legitimately claim to work in a rights-based, consultative, or participatory manner, because its programmes may not only exclude disabled women, men, and children, but actively reinforce their disadvantage and marginalisation in society.

The need for a gender analysis

Disabled people are not a homogeneous group. Disabled men and women may have interests in common, but they also have experiences, interests, and needs which differ. Policies and interventions, such as supporting disabled people's organisations, which appear to be 'gender-neutral' — in other words claiming to apply to men and women equally — may in fact be supporting one group of people while ignoring, or operating at the expense of, another group or individual. Disability programmes, like all programmes, need to be overlaid with a gender analysis at every stage.

Why a gender analysis?

The word 'gender' is often mistakenly understood to mean 'women's issues', and the phrase 'gender analysis' to mean 'work with women'.

Men and women in different societies take on different roles, which are socially, rather than biologically, assigned to them. In many societies, domestic work is regarded as 'women's work', even though there is no biological reason why it should not be equally the responsibility of men. Similarly, fighting is often seen as 'men's duty'. In some societies, collecting firewood is 'men's work'; in others it is a task for women or for both sexes. A gender analysis, examining these socially ascribed roles and the way in which power and choices are distributed between men and women, is a crucial element in any vulnerability analysis. It cannot be assumed that men and women living in the same household or employed in the same work-place have equal scope for choice and control in their lives. One person in a household may have greater access to and control over resources and may, for example, be relatively well nourished, while others in the same household are under-nourished.

A gender analysis will look not only at the different social roles of men and women but also at how those roles are perceived and valued by society, and at the social structures which frame and influence those values and perceptions.

Frequently such an analysis shows that women are vulnerable and dis-advantaged relative to men of the same class, with a lower value placed on 'female' contributions to society.

In the light of gender analyses, the interventions of relief and development agencies often seek specifically to support women in their efforts to bring about change in their lives, because women and girls usually have the poorest access to health care, employment, education/literacy, and so on. For example: for an urban male wheelchair-user in Bosnia, access to public buildings may be just as limited as it is for a displaced rural female wheelchair-user (or a wheelchair-user who is a well-paid expatriate aid worker), but the former is likely to be better placed in terms of local connections, access to employment, representation through a local association of disabled people, and the social/ political advantages of being male in his society. A development agency may decide to support both people in lobbying the authorities on issues of access, but may also decide to offer further support to the displaced woman in her efforts to challenge structures which disproportionately discriminate against her in comparison with the man, who may actually be part of those structures.

The fact that gender analysis often leads to interventions which target women leads to the mistaken understanding that gender = women. However, a gender analysis is not simply about designing interventions to work with women, but also about ensuring that *any* intervention takes account of the social roles of men and women and does not support one group of people to the detriment of another.

Roles of men and women during and after conflict

War may affect men and women in different ways; aspects of their social roles may be transformed, reinforced, or polarised in the process.

In Bosnia, the vast majority of those mobilised into the army were men, who thus extended their social roles as protectors of their families. These men were exposed to the stress and fear of frontline fighting, to the physical hardships, tensions, boredom, and restricted freedoms of military service, to the risk of death and physical injury, and to mental and physical abuse in detention centres and prisoner-of-war camps. Those not mobilised lived in constant fear of the draft. Elderly, ill, and disabled men had to live with the frustration of being unable to fulfil one aspect of their socially ascribed 'male' role.

Women — many of whom, besides managing their households, were engaged in paid employment before the war or were involved in subsistence farming and agriculture — became increasingly responsible for day-to-day household decision-making and the protection of their families. With men away at the front, killed, missing, displaced, or detained, the task of ensuring the daily survival of family members increasingly fell to women. Women took on extra responsibilities for supplementing community services such as education, health care, and support for vulnerable members of the community. The collapse of welfare services had particularly profound effects on the daily lives of women and disabled people.

The value which society ascribes to the contributions of men during war is higher than that which it ascribes to those of women. While men's suffering is evident, women's social roles in war-time are less visible and a less dramatic extension of their pre-war roles. On the other hand, conflict may offer women opportunities to advance their interests as a social group. As they organise themselves to campaign on issues such as the fate of missing people or the supply of relief items to soldiers, they emerge into public and political arenas opened up during conflict, and their roles may be transformed.

When the war is over, they may lose ground on other fronts. In Bosnia, for example,the directors of free-market enterprises are unlikely to reinstate the pre-war provision of work-place facilities such as creches and gynaecological units which had been attached to State-run factories. Similarly, women and disabled people are likely to encounter discrimination in the labour market and may be relegated back to their homes: fears of the social unrest which may be stirred up by under-occupied ex-soldiers, coupled with a sense of obligation to war veterans, may mean that demobilised men, returning to the role of family protectors and providers, are given priority in the queue for scarce jobs.

In Bosnia, Oxfam acknowledged and tried to respond to the immediate needs of the whole community while hostilities lasted, but its analyses predicted that in the long term some people stood to lose more than others. Those identified as especially vulnerable included women and disabled people who lacked social-support networks. Accordingly, Oxfam gave a high priority to interventions designed to support these particular groups.

Gender analysis in disability work

While disabled women may have concerns in common with other women and with disabled men, and disabled men may have concerns in common with other men and with disabled women, their identity cannot be simply broken down into single categories. They will have their own distinct experiences, not only as 'disabled' and as 'women' or 'men', but as 'disabled women' or 'disabled men' — each of whom in addition will have other identities created by their ethnicity, regional affiliation, rural or urban background, and so on.

Disabled women may identify concerns and obstacles which are different from those which affect disabled men or non-disabled women. This can be seen in the analysis produced by disabled women in the Lotos Centre, reported in Chapter 6. It is often true that a disabled man can rely on female relatives for domestic and personal support, while a disabled woman may not only be deprived of such support, but may find herself having to provide it for a disabled or non-disabled partner. The gender-determined division of labour in a given society may have profound implications for the life-chances of disabled boys and girls. In a society where women are expected to take a primarily domestic role and men to take a public role and enter the labour market, a disabled boy may receive more encouragement to fulfil his physical and educational potential than a girl, destined for a role which is less socially valued. Development agencies need to find ways of ensuring that disabled women are consulted about their particular concerns, so that interventions can be designed to support them, not to make their problems worse. Agencies should beware of assuming that male community leaders represent the interests and concerns of women.

Similarly, disabled men may have concerns distinct from those of non-disabled men and disabled women. It may be harder for them than for non-disabled men, for example, to find paid employment. Besides the obvious problems of daily survival, this may leave a disabled man unable to fulfil a social role as provider and protector of his family, and this may diminish his self-respect and social status.

In Bosnia, Oxfam realised the need to consider the gender-conditioned effects of the social model of disability. Community-based care is the preference of most disabled people, but it must be properly resourced to ensure that individual carers, the majority of whom are women, are not obliged to subsidise the State and community with an increased work-load. The Koraci Nade Centre supported parents not only by training them in child-management, but by encouraging contact between them and enabling them and their children to have time apart from each other.

A well-developed advocacy strategy on disability issues, informed by a gender analysis, will stress that resources must be made available to support women, who constitute the majority of carers: it is essential to ensure that disabled people do not gain their rights at the expense of other family members. The strategy should also stress the provision of enabling aids and services (such as child-care assistance for disabled parents) to ensure that disabled people, women in particular, can carry out their domestic tasks. The development of services such as transport, day centres, relief nurses/carers, accessible health services, and so on is central to this approach.

The case for an institutional policy on disability

As with gender issues, the organisation itself is the starting point for developing work on disability, and for ensuring that all programming is subject to a disability analysis. A development agency needs first to look hard at its own practices, structures, staffing, and policy, to see what factors may block disabled people from participating. This initial self-analysis is indispensable. Any agency hoping to be effective in working with disabled people needs to clarify its aims and values to itself, its staff, partners, and counterparts.

Oxfam's staff involved in Eastern Europe and the Former Soviet Union concluded that it is essential to have a *policy* on disability which clearly states the organisation's approach and frames its expectations of its staff and programmes. The policy should address both internal practice and external service-provision. It would provide a basis on which people inside and outside the organisation could take issue with the institution if it did not fulfil its stated commitments. It would *oblige* managers to ensure that their programmes incorporated a disability analysis, and that staff developed positive attitudes to disability. It would support managers who had to make difficult decisions about resource allocation — for example, choosing between physical modifications to an office and some other urgent need.

Managers need to be properly supported if they are to implement a disability policy. Employing disabled staff may incur extra costs, and resources should be allocated for this contingency. Large organisations may want to consider establishing a central fund to enable disabled staff to do their jobs. Field managers would not then have to make difficult choices between financing the implementation of equal-opportunities recruitment procedures against other programme priorities, or feel that the expenditure required justification beyond reference to the policy.

At the root of the social disadvantages and oppression experienced by disabled people lie discrimination, fear, and prejudice. Challenging negative attitudes within an organisation needs a long-term, consistent approach, supported by daily management. It begins with institution-wide policies and mandate, and should be central to the smallest initiative and practice of the most remote field office. Implementation of a disability policy needs to be supported by a structured programme of training, for which resources and expertise will be required.

While there can be no overnight results in these constantly dynamic processes of personal and organisational analysis of practice and attitude, an acceptable limit needs to be set. Oxfam found it important to make attitude to disability a key criterion when recruiting new staff in Bosnia. An individual's philosophy and beliefs should broadly match those of the organisation, in order for both to be effective. To make some assessment of this, it is helpful to articulate a clear policy position which defines the organisation's own stance.

It can be seen within Oxfam that lack of such clarity can lead to inconsistencies. Oxfam's work with disabled people is well developed in some areas and non-existent in others; there is a lack of consistency even within regions, and a very palpable lack of resources and knowledge within the institution for taking this work forward. Although some progress has been made, Oxfam does not yet have a Disability Policy.

The support of the UK-based Disability Adviser, who was subsequently replaced by three field-based disability advisers, was essential to the development of disability work in Eastern Europe and the former Soviet Union. Her input in training, offering advice, developing a dialogue with field staff, networking, and identifying resources gave the Tuzla team, and others in the region, the confidence to initiate work with various groups of disabled people. Her appointment, however, reflected not a general policy to develop disability work, but the commitment of one particular senior manager in the head office, who gave a high priority to finding resources for the post.

As Oxfam's experience in Tuzla illustrates, in the initial stages a small group of staff members may need to take forward work on disability; but this process needs careful management, to avoid a separatist approach and to ensure that disability is integrated into the whole programme. To encourage team involvement, staff could be seconded from different areas into a working group which might consist, for example, of a logistician, an administrator, a driver, a water engineer, and a relief coordinator, as well as staff specifically working on social development. The participation of disabled people is essential in any such group. If there are no disabled staff members, disabled people from partner organisations and target groups could be invited to act as advisers.

If the staff team consists entirely of non-disabled people, the organisation needs to ask itself why. The implementation of equal-opportunities procedures may be a step towards disability equity, but not all people start from an equal position and cannot therefore compete for employment on an equal basis. A field evaluation and analysis of the cultural and social factors which add to the disadvantages of disabled people in the external environment may lead to the adoption of positive-action strategies such as trainee posts or mentoring.

In Former Yugoslavia, Oxfam made contractual commitments to disabled staff which clearly outlined the resources that would be made available to ensure that staff members could do their jobs. Each contract was individually negotiated to take account of individual impairments. It was intended that staff members would know clearly (and if necessary be able to refer to) the support they could expect as of right, while managers would be able to budget for any extra costs. In practice, without access to central or additional funds to supplement the field-office budget, the recruitment of disabled staff members might be blocked by shortage of funds, obliging managers to make impossible choices. To avoid this situation, when development agencies are doing forward planning and applying for external funds, they should take account of the predicted financial costs of removing barriers for disabled staff. In turn, donor organisations would need to ensure that their budgeting and prioritisation policies were subject to a disability analysis.

The need for planning and analysis

Although conflicts and other emergencies are by their very nature unpredictable, some degree of planning and analysis is necessary. For Oxfam Tuzla, short-term funding led not only to short-term contracts and job insecurity, but also, when dealing with matters like the employment of disabled staff, to the improvisation of plans in a very *ad hoc* fashion.

One reason was the nature of the available funding. Large donors tend to have emergency funds set aside for rapid responses, managed separately from the deployment of development funds. Until donors recognise the need for a unified approach in their grant allocations and internal administration, and acknowledge from empirical evidence that emergencies have long-term effects, this situation is likely to continue.

Working in conflict brings with it specific challenges and threats. Besides taking account of the obvious physical risks, NGOs must consider other factors which can have a serious effect on a development programme: disrupted communications, constraints on transport and freedom of movement, logistical constraints on the purchase of supplies, limited access to information, obstructive border controls, customs barriers, limited banking facilities, and devaluation of currency — to name only a few.

For Oxfam in Bosnia, the strategic planning process proved very useful in determining overall visions for the field work. This helped staff to keep their aims in focus, despite the difficulties created by short-term funding. In the context of war, the challenge to think strategically was extremely difficult, but nevertheless general directions and approaches as well as specific interventions could be identified, and this helped staff to remain committed to their work during the very bleakest times.

In a context where the situation could develop in many unpredictable directions, Oxfam found that the use of scenario planning made it possible to work with a staff team, project staff, and partners to identify possible future changes in the external environment. From that point it could be made clear how the organisation was likely to act or react in any situation. This included defining at what point a programme might be closed down; what type of event would be considered an unacceptable security risk; when and how staff would be evacuated; and who would be eligible for evacuation. This allowed all those involved in the programme to be clear about their expectations of the organisation, and to be more effective in their response when a particular event occurred.

The Koraci Nade project suffered from a lack of practical planning in the initial stages, and specifically from the lack of long-term funding. Even a pilot project needs funding — not only for the pilot period, but to help it to identify possible sponsors for the future. Ideally, before beginning a project, clear aims and objectives should be identified, so that on-going monitoring and evaluation can take place. This type of planning does not have to be rigid; indeed, it is better to allow for a changing situation.

Planning can be used to ensure flexibility; for example, the outreach component of Koraci Nade became very important when an escalation of fighting forced the Centre to close. The strength of any programme in an extreme situation is its ability to adapt to an unpredictable and ever-changing environment.

At the same time, while short-termism made progress and planning difficult, it did not make it impossible. From the project-management point of view, some tough decisions had to be made, even before the Centre opened. Oxfam Tuzla had been approached by a potential implementing partner looking for funding. Instead of agreeing to fund a project which it felt to be incompatible with its own approach, Oxfam chose to run its own operational project. In many ways this is contrary to the Oxfam ethos; but undoubtedly it was the most appropriate way forward in this case, even if it did create external tensions and problems for the project at later stages.

While long-term funding was a real problem from the outset, a judgement had to be made on the best course of action. Two and a half years later, such funding has still not been identified, but options for ensuring sustainability have been defined. If the implementation of the project had been delayed until long-term funding was found, it might not have happened at all, and Oxfam and its partners would not now be in a position to capitalise on opportunities for advocacy. The risks involved in beginning a project that may not be sustainable, raising unfounded expectations and hopes, have to be weighed against the risks of doing nothing at all.

From charity to change: new opportunities and the role of advocacy

Oxfam's experience in Bosnia shows that it is essential for a development agency to develop internal systems and internal consistency if it is to do effective work in partnership with disabled people. Part of that work will inevitably involve advocacy activities, and the messages given out by the organisation at all levels should be consistent with the implementation of its projects in the field.

The 'one programme' approach

As an organisation, Oxfam works on the principle of a unified programme, stressing that relief, development, and advocacy interventions are not separable stages, between which there has to be a linear progression over time. While any particular intervention, depending on the context, may be weighted more towards relief, development, or advocacy strategies, the intention of the one-programme approach is to maximise impact both immediately and in the long-term future.

For example, it has been noted that the random distribution of relief items in an emergency can further marginalise some groups of people, which can create conditions which block later work with a greater emphasis on social development. Agencies need to analyse in advance how emergency-relief interventions might in themselves form part of a longer-term development strategy — for example, by stimulating community organisation through the creation of representative committees from a displaced community. It is important to ensure that the representation reflects the multiple identities of people in the community, and in this way strengthen the future capacity of vulnerable people to organise and represent themselves.

Oxfam has found that, in emergencies, provision for immediate needs has to be balanced with longer-term strategies for addressing the causes of vulnerability and poverty. Because the effects of emergencies are long-lasting, sustainable responses need to be developed. The factors which cause or exacerbate emergencies and make people vulnerable to disasters need long-term analysis and action, not improvised and unconsidered responses.

Thus emergency-relief and development work are intrinsically linked — and institutional divisions between departments responsible for each kind of response need to be broken down. The knowledge and experience of a culture, society, area, and people which long-term development staff possess or acquire are no less essential in an emergency than the technical skills and special abilities of disaster-relief personnel. In their response to the needs of vulnerable people in emergencies, all relief and development workers need to treat disability as an issue for immediate priority, and not something which can be addressed at a later stage.

Simultaneously, to maximise the impact of interventions, opportunities for advocacy need to be identified and acted on at every stage. Whereas a single project or intervention may significantly benefit a specific group of people, its impact is necessarily finite. A 'multiplier' effect is produced by combining it with an advocacy strategy with defined aims, clear strategies for achieving them, and specific roles and targets identified.

The aims of an advocacy strategy should coincide with those of relief and development work on the same issues. This can happen at various levels. For example, in an emergency distribution of relief items, while some field staff may be physically distributing the goods and lobbying other agencies on-site to provide certain services identified as lacking, others may be negotiating with other agencies or local authorities for emergency accommodation to be made accessible for disabled people, or for people to be rehoused in a safer environment; at the same time, the staff at head office may be lobbying donor agencies to respond, members of parliament to address political root causes, and the media to ensure that the situation is not forgotten. The efforts of field and head offices can be combined by, for example, inviting influential public figures to visit the site of the crisis and publicise identified issues for debate.

Advocacy and Koraci Nade

In reality, developing a coordinated programme in a complex emergency can be difficult, but investment in planning can yield later benefits and avoid mistakes. The case of Koraci Nade illustrates this. On the one hand, short-termism in funding and forward planning hampered the early development of a coordinated one-programme strategy, which subsequently gave rise to problems; on the other hand, longer-term aims such as introducing the social model of disability and community-based approaches to child development were always fundamental to the project: they were clear from the outset, and informed later advocacy initiatives.

The Centre was originally set up in response to a complete lack of provision for disabled children and their parents in a crisis. With longer-term aims identified, immediate needs had to be met: shoes and clothing were distributed to children attending the Centre. Strategically, this had two advantages: it supplied some of the children's urgent physical needs, while at the same time providing an incentive to attend at the Centre, and thus giving the staff a chance to prove to children and wary parents the value of their fundamentally different approach.

The longer-term prospects for the Centre and for other children in the Tuzla region have been fundamentally influenced by advocacy initiatives at multiple levels. There are many examples of this. At a personal level, staff from ZID joined with Koraci Nade staff to lobby for a child to be allowed to attend school.

The direct involvement of students and staff from the Defectology Faculty equipped them to advocate the Koraci Nade model and social approach in numerous institutions in Bosnia-Hercegovina. Oxfam joined together with other concerned agencies to raise issues of community-based care with the 'expert group' and other sectors of the international community. At the Lotos Centre, an advocacy base for disabled adults was developed, to help them to lobby and campaign locally and nationally on issues of policy that affect the lives of children at Koraci Nade and also in other areas of Bosnia. Oxfam staff lobbied reconstruction agencies and donors on issues of access, to try to ensure that schools in future will be accessible to disabled children, so that they can start on the path to full integration in society. As the result of a close relationship between Oxfam and the Italian Red Cross, the Kosta Popov School project, funded by the IRC, is the first (and potentially very influential) example of an accessible construction project, and one where the social and community implications have been considered very carefully by the construction agency.

Post-war advocacy opportunities for disabled people in Bosnia

Advocacy has a crucial role to play in the post-war period in Bosnia. A system is evolving which will allow parents and disabled people to play a much stronger role in defining future services. An independent NGO sector is emerging in the space that has opened up between the State and individuals in the community. It is at an embryonic stage, but the opportunities offered by a multi-party political system are becoming apparent to community groups and grassroots organisations.

While the mass presence of international relief agencies in Bosnia during the war created a distorted impression of NGOs as primarily institutions charged with delivering 'humanitarian aid', it has also helped to stimulate and accelerate the growth of the local NGO sector. The potential problems of an entirely donor-led NGO sector must be acknowledged, but the spontaneous growth of people's and community organisations, followed by the development of a legal framework, offers opportunities for disabled people to organise themselves and lobby the authorities.

The destruction of pre-war institutions, infrastructure, and systems has created a gap in provision which, for all the problems which it caused during the fighting, now offers an opportunity, as reconstruction begins, for disabled people to campaign for the services they really want and thus gain greater control over their lives and futures. Evidently, conflict can act as a catalyst, and positive change can be achieved through advocacy.

Organisations which represent disabled people are becoming more democratic and more politicised, and there is a general shift from administering charity to catalysing change. Their full potential has not yet been realised, and some are still building the capacity and confidence required for the transition to a campaigning role. To an external observer it seems obvious that disabled people could gain strength by uniting under one umbrella to demand change. It is difficult to predict how a united front of disabled people will respond to the tensions which prevail between pre-war disabled people, war veterans, and war-disabled civilians; but, given the opportunity, war-disabled people may bring a fresh wind of change to the traditional associations of disabled people.

The need to be prepared

At times during the conflict, the difficulties of applying the principles of the social model of disability to the Koraci Nade project seemed insurmountable. However, it is in the arena of advocacy that we can see most clearly the importance of supporting the development of local organisations of disabled people, and of introducing alternative approaches to disability *during* the war.

Drawing on lessons learnt from the advance of disability movements elsewhere, the Oxfam Tuzla staff always believed that real change would happen only when disabled people themselves organised and demanded it. As well as implementing operational projects like Koraci Nade and campaigning and lobbying on relevant issues, the team identified a role for Oxfam in supporting networks between disabled people, helping them to build their own capacity and strategies for advocacy.

It is probably true that, if Oxfam Tuzla had not begun to work with disabled children, adults, carers, medical professionals, and other agencies during the war, initially in emergency interventions, those now involved in Koraci Nade and Lotos would be at a very different stage of organisation and discussion and would still be responding to disability solely on the principles of the 'medical model'. They would be less organised to lobby on issues of post-war reconstruction, and less able to have an influence over their futures at a time which presents a crucial opportunity to do so. Hence the importance of supporting the development of local organisations during the emergency phase, so that they are ready to represent themselves at the opportune moment, with strategies and ideas clearly formulated in advance.

Oxfam Tuzla has found that its operations in the field during the war have brought both benefits and problems. On the one hand, an international agency must build its credibility before being able to do effective advocacy work, and field-work during an emergency can prove strategically useful later on: Oxfam is now an established presence and is likely to be consulted by policy-makers. On the other hand, the introduction of radical approaches has alienated Oxfam from some influential policy-makers, and the damage is proving difficult to repair.

One of the key problems for Oxfam was how to work with local authorities without usurping their role. In the initial stages of Koraci Nade this was not a significant issue, because the authorities were not in a position to offer any kind of service to disabled children. But the lack of a constructive relationship at the early stages later proved to be a major obstacle to Oxfam's attempts to merge Koraci Nade with local-authority services.

This lack of co-operation with local services has been counter-balanced only partly by the positive development of parental roles. For the most severely disabled children, their parents are their main advocates. The family, however, is not automatically the healthiest environment for the child, nor are parents automatically the best advocates of the rights of the child. Oxfam found that parents and professionals needed training on basic-rights issues, and also needed to work more closely with disabled adults (which would have the added advantage of providing the children with positive role models). The role played by Koraci Nade in educating and informing parents about their children's impairments and potential has not only challenged myths about disability, but also made parents stronger and more effective advocates on their behalf.

Learning from each other

In introducing the social model of disability in Bosnia, Oxfam was importing a new concept of the rights of disabled people, the obligations of government, and the role of professionals. It was ambitious to attempt this in a society which was not only in transition from collectivist values, but embroiled in a devastating war. But the conflict also offered opportunities, such as the breakdown of the institutional system, which meant that many parents and children who otherwise would not have done so experienced Koraci Nade's community-based way of working. Non-disabled children were able to play with and learn from disabled children with whom they otherwise might never have had contact.

The international presence in Bosnia has also brought about changes, both positive and negative. Bosnian people have had the chance to experience a whole range of approaches to social and community issues from many countries around the world. This offers a great opportunity for learning from the mistakes and successes of others and developing an approach appropriate to the Bosnian context.

In order to promote the social model of disability, it was necessary to address not only problems such as social and institutional discrimination, but also the practical methods of professional work. The staff of Koraci Nade have described how difficult it was for them to adapt to play-therapy with groups. The single most effective factor in achieving change was the on-going daily involvement in the project by staff familiar with a community-based approach. In combination with the recruitment of project staff open to trying new ideas, and the prolonged time-period of the training, this has proved very effective.

In the case of Koraci Nade, these interactions could have been undermined had the project become prematurely independent of Oxfam. Oxfam felt it crucially important to ensure that the Centre had addressed the issue of integration before plans were laid for independence. The organisation could have lost all its influence before the new ideas had had time to prove themselves and be accepted by the disabled children, their parents, and the professionals. While Oxfam was keen to ensure a sustainable future for the Centre, cutting loose a flawed project or one that had not built capacity for survival would do nothing to meet identified aims.

During all this time, Oxfam itself has been able to learn from its interaction with the parents, children, and staff at Koraci Nade, and this book represents one way of sharing the learning and benefits of those contacts with the wider development community.

The future of the Koraci Nade Centre

The war in Bosnia has had a devastating affect on the Bosnian people. Much of the information and experiences included in this book have come from the Federation experience, simply because the Koraci Nade project and the people associated with it are from the Federation Entity. But the challenges faced by disabled people in the Republika Srpska are the same, or even greater in some areas, where significantly less funding has been available for support and reconstruction.

As in all emergency situations, there will not be a neat ending point, when everything will be resolved and 'normal' again. After such a terrible war and years of international presence, no country could ever be exactly the same again. Now that there is relative peace in Bosnia, many changes are apparent.

The potential of the Koraci Nade Centre represents one of the more positive prospects for the future in Bosnia. The Overseas Development Administration of the British government has committed a further £100,000 to support the continued development of the Oxfam Tuzla disability programme in 1997. This has enabled Oxfam staff to continue negotiations with the Kosta Popov School and the local authorities to secure the long-term future of the Centre; through phased integration into local structures, it should become part of the statutory provision for disabled children. Oxfam is supported in this by the parents and by some local professionals, who want to see the Centre integrated into the school.

If negotiations are successful, and the integrative rights-based approach to the education and support of disabled children is implemented within existing educational structures, the children, staff, and parents of Koraci Nade will have a unique opportunity to play a role in defining future services for disabled children in Bosnia. The ODA funding also ensures that the children and parents of Koraci Nade will be further supported by the provision of enabling aids from the ZID workshop, and by the advocacy potential of the disabled adults of the Lotos Centre.

Despite all the problems, which at times led to despair that integration would ever be possible, the Koraci Nade Centre has proved to be a very successful project, and one which could be an important model for future service-provision in Bosnia. Since the peace agreement, long-term planning has become much more of a possibility, in both practical and psychological terms. The staff of Koraci Nade now see a clear way forward, and the Centre Coordinator, Ajsa Mahmuglagic, says that there has never been a more hopeful time in the Centre's history:

❧ I am optimistic about the future of the Centre. The local authorities now realise the needs of these children and have made a promise to keep the Centre open. With Oxfam's help, and in co-operation with the Association of Mothers, Kosta Popov School, and the Faculty of Defectology, we will work together as one team. We all have the same aim: that the Centre continues to work and that this approach becomes bigger and wider in Bosnia. These children must have their place in the sun, too. ❧

Further reading

This section contains suggestions for further reading about the main themes of this book. The inclusion of any title in the list does not necessarily imply that its analysis is endorsed by Oxfam.

About Bosnia

Misha Glenny: *The Fall of Yugoslavia: The Third Balkan War* (London, Penguin, 1992)

Noel Malcolm: *Bosnia — A Short History* (London: Macmillan, 1994)

Laura Silber and Allan Little: *The Death of Yugoslavia* (London: Penguin, 1995)

Ed Vulliamy: *Seasons in Hell: Understanding Bosnia's War* (London: Simon and Schuster, 1994)

About disability rights and the social model of disability

C. Barnes and G. Mercer: 'Disability: emancipation, community participation, and disabled people' in M. Mayo and G. Craig (eds.): *Community Empowerment: A Reader in Participation and Development* (London: Zed Books, 1995)

E. Boylan: *Women and Disability* (London: Zed Books, 1991)

Jane Campbell and Michael Oliver: *Disability Politics* (London: Routledge, 1996)

Peter Coleridge: *Disability, Liberation, and Development* (Oxford: Oxfam UK and Ireland, 1993)

Diane Dredger: *The Last Civil Rights Movement* (London: Hurst and Co., 1989)

Einer Helander: *Prejudice and Dignity: An Introduction to Community-Based Rehabilitation* (New York: United Nations, 1993)

B. Ingstad and S. Reynolds White: *Disability and Culture* (University of California Press, 1995)

International Labour Organisation: *Community-Based Rehabilitation For and With People With Disabilities* (Geneva: ILO, 1994)

Jenny Morris: *Pride Against Prejudice* (London: Women's Press, 1991)

Jenny Morris: *Encounters with Strangers* (London: Women's Press, 1996)

Michael Oliver: *Understanding Disability* (London: Macmillan, 1996)

Brian O'Toole and Roy McConkey (eds.): *Innovations in Developing Countries for People with Disabilities* (Chorley, Lancs: Lisieux Hall, 1995)

Save the Children: *Disability and Overseas Programmes: Current situation and future options for Save the Children* (London, SCF UK, 1993)

About working with disabled children

Naomi Richman: *Helping Children in Difficult Circumstances: A Teacher's Manual* (London, SCF UK, 1991)

Naomi Richman: *Communicating with Children: Helping Children in Distress* (London, SCF UK, 1993)

Naomi Richman: *Principles of Help for Children Involved in Organised Violence* (London, SCF UK, 1996)

Marigold Thorburn et al.: *Practical Approaches to Childhood Disability in Developing Countries: Insights from Experience and Research* (from 3D Projects, 14 Monk Street, Spanish Town, Jamaica)

Save the Children: *Children, Disability, and Development: Achievement and Challenge* (London: SCF, 1994) – with accompanying manual and 72-minute video

Save the Children: *Observing Children Playing* (video and handbook) (London: SCF, 1994)

David Werner: *Disabled Village Children: A Guide for Community Workers, Rehabilitation Workers and Families* (Palo Alto, CA: The Hesperian Foundation, 1987)

Pam Zinkin and Helen McConachie: *Disabled Children and Developing Countries* (London: MacKeith Press, 1985)

About development work in the context of armed conflict

Mark Adams and Mark Bradbury: *Conflict and Development: Organisational Adaptation in Conflict Situations* (Oxford: Oxfam UK and Ireland, 1995)

K.M. Cahill (ed.): *A Framework for Survival: Health, Human Rights, and Humanitarian Assistance in Conflicts and Disasters* (New York: Basic Books)

Michael Cranna (ed): *The True Cost of Conflict* (London: Earthscan, 1994)

F. Jean: *Populations in Danger: Médecins Sans Frontières* (London: John Libbey, 1993)

Mark Cutts and A. Dingle: *Safety First: Protecting NGO Employees Who Work in Areas of Conflict* (London: SCF, 1995)

Larry Minear and Thomas G. Weiss: *Mercy Under Fire* (Boulder: Westview, 1995)

Shawn Roberts and Jody Williams: *After the Guns Fall Silent: The Enduring Legacy of Landmines* (Washington DC: Vietnam Veterans of America Foundation, 1995)

Geoff Tansey et al.: *A World Divided* (London: Earthscan, 1994)

Thomas G. Weiss and Larry Minear: *Humanitarian Action in Times of War* (London: Lynne Rienner, 1993)

Thomas G. Weiss and Larry Minear: *Humanitarianism Across Borders: Sustaining Civilians in Times of War* (London: Lynne Rienner, 1993)

Journals and magazines

Disability and Society, a quarterly journal published by Carfax Publishing Company, PO Box 25, Abingdon, OX14 3UE, England.

Disasters: The Journal of Disaster Studies and Management, published quarterly by Blackwell Publishers, 108 Cowley Road, Oxford, OX4 1JH, England.

Journal of Humanitarian Affairs, published electronically by the University of Cambridge (http://www-jha.sps.cam.ac.uk/

Vox Nostra, published quarterly by Disabled People's International, 101-7 Evergreen Place, Winnipeg, Mb., Canada R3L 2T3

Oxfam Development Casebooks

● empowering communities
A Casebook from West Sudan

Peter Strachan and Chris Peters
An account of the Kebkabiya project,
which began as an attempt to improve
food security in the wake of a major
famine. Oxfam initially managed all the
project activities, but now responsibility
has been largely transferred to a
community-based organisation.

The account of the increasing
involvement of the community, and
the creation of democratic structures
for managing the project, provides
valuable insights into the way in which
a participative approach to development can result in empowerment
for communities.

0 85598 358 2

UK and Ireland

**Oxfam (UK and Ireland) publishes a wide range of books, manuals, and
resource materials for specialist, academic, and general readers.**

For a free catalogue, please write to:
Oxfam Publishing,
274 Banbury Road,
Oxford OX2 7DZ, UK;
telephone (0)1865 313922
e-mail publish@oxfam.org.uk

Oxfam publications are available from the following agents:

for Canada and the USA: Humanities Press International, 165 First Avenue, Atlantic
Highlands, New Jersey NJ 07716-1289, USA; tel. (908) 872 1441; fax (908) 872 0717

or southern Africa: David Philip Publishers, PO Box 23408, Claremont, Cape Town 7735,
South Africa; tel. (021) 64 4136; fax (021) 64 3358.